STRATEGIC PLANNING

STRATEGIC PLANNING

An Interactive Process for Leaders

Dan R. Ebener
and
Frederick L. Smith

Paulist Press
New York / Mahwah, NJ

Drawing on p. 118 by Frank Sabatté
Cover image by Ali Mazraie Shadi / Shutterstock.com
Cover design by Sharyn Banks
Book design by Lynn Else

Library of Congress Cataloging-in-Publication Data

Ebener, Dan R., author.
    Strategic planning : an interactive process for leaders / Dan R. Ebener and Frederick L. Smith.
        pages cm
    Includes bibliographical references.
    ISBN 978-0-8091-4920-9 (pbk. : alk. paper) — ISBN 978-1-58768-484-5 (e book)
    1. Strategic planning. 2. Leadership. I. Smith, Frederick L., author. II. Title.
    HD30.28.E24 2015
    658.4'012—dc23

                                                                        2014050160

ISBN 978-0-8091-4920-9 (paperback)
ISBN 978-1-58768-484-5 (e-book)

Published by Paulist Press
997 Macarthur Boulevard
Mahwah, New Jersey 07430

www.paulistpress.com

Printed and bound in the
United States of America

CONTENTS

FOREWORD
Leading Strategic Change

As the world gets busier and the pace of change swirls around us, it is easy to get caught up in the day-to-day crises and dismiss the need for strategic thinking and planning. Yet those very crises that demand our attention make it even more important that we as leaders create a sense of urgency about vision, strategy, and the process described in this book.

As CEO, I could just sit down and write a strategic plan for Family Resources. In fact, that would make the process much faster and easier. But then it would be my plan, and only my plan. It wouldn't go anywhere. No one would get excited about it—as people do when you involve them.

My position of authority offers me the opportunity to make strategic decisions on my own. But I realize that leadership is not a position. One of the unique contributions of this book is making that distinction between leadership and positions of authority so we can see how as leaders, we need to involve others in an *interactive* process.

From personal experience, I can recommend the strategic planning process described in this book. In fact, strategic planning —as described here—has offered me the opportunity for some of the most interactive experiences of my career. This book describes a process where leaders and members of an organization take initiative and work together to change something.

I have seen how the process described in this book can involve literally hundreds of people in the planning process, thereby building a sense of ownership among many more people whose buy-in we need. It gets people excited about the change we are trying to lead.

My hope is that this book can provide assistance to anyone looking to involve many others in the interactive process that strategic planning can be.

Cheryl Goodwin
CEO, Family Resources, Inc.

PREFACE

As teachers and practitioners of strategic planning, we have long been looking for a textbook for our courses and a guidebook for our consulting work that approaches strategic planning from a more comprehensive perspective. Our search for a book that approaches strategic planning from a leadership perspective, as well as covering *all three* sectors of society—businesses, not-for-profits, and public entities—inspired us to write this book.

Most strategic planning books are written for not-for-profit (charitable) groups and public (governmental) organizations. We believe that the interactive process in this book can apply to all three social sectors—including businesses. In fact, we know it can work because we have used this process with many groups from all three sectors.

It is the content of strategy, not the strategic planning process itself, that differs between the three sectors. The for-profit sector requires more attention to the competitive nature of business. The not-for-profit sector requires more collaboration among similar groups. The public sector has to respond to more public scrutiny. However, we believe the process of planning strategically is essentially the same.

Our students and clients tell us that books on strategic planning are too difficult to read and understand. They tell us they are not interested in becoming experts in the field so much as practitioners of strategy for their own organizations. They want a book they can read, understand, and put into practice.

After twenty years of searching for the right book, we finally answered the call of our students, clients, and colleagues by writing our own.

This book emphasizes the role of leaders in the strategic planning process. Most books on strategic planning assume that leadership is positional and that strategic planning is the purview of people in positions of authority. We take a different view.

We believe strategic planning is a conversation that takes place between leaders, followers, and managers about the direction that an organization needs to take. In strategic planning, members of an organization interact with each other, explore alternatives together, and discover a shared vision that can take the organization in a new direction.

Strategic planning is an interactive process where leaders, followers, and managers create a common goal together. Interaction is important to both the process and content of leadership. We hope that the interactive process we describe here can provide (1) opportunities for various groups to engage more actively in strategic change efforts, and (2) a meaningful way for people to practice the art of organizational leadership.

Our process is simple—and therefore we tried to keep this book simple. Strategic planning does not have to be complicated. We break it down to eight steps:

1. Get the right people at the table.
2. Do your homework in advance.
3. Focus on your mission and values.
4. Prioritize your most strategic areas of concern.
5. Generate new and creative ideas to address these issues.
6. Take specific steps that can be measured.
7. Communicate your new vision clearly.
8. Hold yourself accountable by implementing the strategic plan.

INTRODUCTION

Strategic Leadership

"If you don't like something, change it."
—Maya Angelou

DEFINING LEADERSHIP AND MANAGEMENT

We define leadership as a voluntary, interactive process where leaders and followers move each other in the direction of a shared vision or a common goal.

The two major factors[1] of leadership are:

1. The task—the strategic change. It is the common goal or shared vision; and
2. The relationship—the social capital. It must be *voluntary and interactive.*

We define strategic planning as one of the interactive processes that moves leaders, managers, and followers toward that shared vision or common goal. In fact, strategic planning helps determine what the common goal is.

Strategic planning and leadership have similar concepts in our definitions: interaction, leaders, followers, and a shared vision or common goal. The art of strategic planning is critical to the success of leaders.

We define management as positional authority that is responsible for organizing structural support for the common goal or shared vision.

The two major factors of management are also:

1. The task—providing structure to the organization; and
2. The relationship—assigning positional roles to organizational members.

Organizations need to be both led *and* managed. Both leadership and management are critical functions for organizational life and for strategic success. And most people in organizations perform both management and leadership roles.

Leadership and management are reciprocal. Efficient management enhances effective leadership and vice versa. Leaders deal with strategy. Managers deal with structure. Organizations need both strategy and structure. Structure requires strategy and strategy needs structure.

Task and Relationship. Differences between leadership and management occur in both the task and the relationship.

The task is measured by whether the job is getting done: Are the goals being met? Are strategies being implemented? Is the mission being accomplished? Is the vision being reached?

The task of managers is to work on operations, focus on day-to-day tasks, and deal with complexity, while leaders work on strategy, focus on longer-range issues, and deal with change.[2]

The relationship is measured by whether the people are motivated: Do they trust those in power? Do they accept their roles? Do they work together? Are they loyal? Are they committed to the mission, vision, and values?

The difference on the relationship side is that management is an authority relationship between managers and their direct reports, while leadership is an influence relationship between leaders and followers.[3]

	Leadership	Management
Task	Change Strategic Planning	Structure Operational Planning
Relationship	Voluntary Interactive	Positional Authority

Figure 1:
The Task and Relationship of Leadership and Management

A common misconception is that leadership is about the relationships and management is about the tasks. "We lead people and manage things," is a common and confusing platitude. That thinking suggests leadership is only concerned about people and not about getting things done. It also assumes that management is only about getting things done and has nothing to do with people. We take a different view: Leaders lead both people and tasks. Managers manage both people and tasks.

STRATEGY, LEADERSHIP, AND MANAGEMENT

Strategy is a task that defines leadership. Strategy is about making progress, moving forward, and creating change. Leaders develop strategy to bring about change. Internal change is necessary to adapt to the changes that are already occurring externally.

Without significant effort to change something, the activity is not leadership.

When you feel passionate about changing something and you invite, inspire, and influence others to join you, you are leading!

Structure is a task that defines management. Managers bring order and stability to organizations. Without structure, order, and stability, people are confused, frustrated, and disinterested. We need structure in our lives, which is the work of managers. We also need life in our structures, which is the work of leaders.

Strategy drives the change that is at the core of leadership. It moves the organization toward the common goal or shared vision upon which leadership is based. Leaders involve people in an interactive process of planning and thinking strategically about the future. In that process, the vision is cocreated by leaders and followers. The vision provides hope by giving people a sense of direction.

These two seemingly contradictory functions—strategy and structure—are the yin and yang of organizational life. Organizations need both. That means they need both leaders and managers. Managers bring structure into our lives and leaders breathe life into those structures.

Strategic planning is at the core of leadership. The world is changing and the pace of change is becoming more and more rapid. In order to anticipate, adjust, and adapt to changes in the environment, leaders plan strategically.

Strategic planning is the formal process that allows an organization to come together and assess the external environment, evaluate the internal workings, and plan accordingly. With a full assessment, leaders, followers, and managers can recalibrate the strategies and design action steps to breathe new life into organizations.

Strategic thinking is the *continuous* process of breathing this new life. It occurs before, during, and after the formal strategic

planning process. Strategic thinking is a skill that can be nur-
tured by reading the signs of the times, reflecting on external
changes in the world, being aware of trends in the business, and
asking, "What major changes are occurring external to my
organization today that will most impact the next three months?
The next three years? The next ten years?" And then, "What can
be done about this now?"

Consider this: *Entropy* is a biological principle that suggests
that every living thing is in the process of dying. This applies to
plants, animals, and yes, each of us as human beings. If we consider that organizations are living organisms—and you should
think of them that way—then they too are in the process of
dying. Organizations need to be revived, restored, and reborn.
External change is constant. Therefore, internal response to these
changes must be proactive and vigilant. The internal response is
our strategy.

In this book, we will describe the interactive, strategic
planning process that we have used with more than 150 organizations. We will share stories from our work that illuminate both
the content and the process of strategic planning for leaders.

We believe the key to our success as strategic planners is
the *interactive process* we both practice and preach. Interaction is
both content *and* process for leadership. As *content*, it is part of
our definition of leadership. As *process*, it makes the difference
between leadership and dictatorship. Without interaction, the
process is not leadership. People in positions of authority can
write a strategic plan without interacting with anyone else. But
that is not leadership.

If leadership is interactive, it involves people. Interaction
brings everyone's ideas out into the open. Leaders and followers
engage in a dialogue, not a monologue. Leaders stimulate task
conflict in order to get different ideas out on the table. Leaders
encourage differences of opinion about how to perform the task.

The feedback we often receive about our interactive process suggests that many people struggle with strategic planning. Sometimes it can be a dictatorial process. It can be a long, boring process. When we facilitate a strategic planning process, we conclude by asking participants to evaluate the experience in one word or phrase. Typically, we hear responses like "lively...motivating... engaging...uplifting...empowering...collaborative...inspiring... energizing..." and "getting everyone on the same page."

People often tell us, "I never knew strategic planning could be so much fun....I wish I had learned this process many years ago....I know another organization that could benefit from this process....Can you work with that organization as well?"

We believe that the key to our success is the *interactive* process outlined next.

THE EBENER-SMITH STRATEGIC PLANNING PROCESS

Step One. Set the Stage: Initiate the Interactive Process. In this step, leaders and managers assemble the strategic planning team. They decide who will take on which roles, what planning steps will be taken, when and how often the strategic planning team will meet, how it will do its homework, and so on. Our role as facilitators is to listen, to explain our model, to offer options, and to allow the organization's members to make the decisions.

Step Two. Do Your Homework: Conduct an Environmental Assessment. This involves gathering the most important data that will inform the strategic planning process. It might include focus groups, interviews, and surveys. It also includes identifying the metrics that are most important for measuring organizational effectiveness.

Step Three. Describe Your Culture: Articulate the Mission and Core Values. Many organizations already have a mission statement. We examine the mission statement to ensure that it has three important features: purpose, business, and values. Fewer organizations have core value statements. We explain our interactive core values process in Step Three.

Step Four. Frame the Questions: Identify the Strategic Areas. These are the major questions, challenges, and issues facing your organization. Defining these issues is often the most important decision made by a strategic planning team. We suggest limiting these issues to three or four. We articulate these issues as questions beginning with *"How can we...?"*

Step Five. Answer the Questions: Develop Strategies. These are possible ways to answer the strategic question that begins with *"How can we...?"* These strategies are not necessarily measurable, but they need to be doable, and within the organization's span of control. Measurability is an important part of the process but it comes later.

Step Six. Get Specific: Write Out the Action Steps. These tangible steps are measurable. We often use action steps that can be measured later by asking: "Was this a go?" Or "Was this a no-go?" Action steps need to be specific enough to be clear on whether the action was taken or not. The group assigns someone to each action item, along with a timeline for when each step will be completed.

Step Seven. Discover the Vision: Craft the Vision Statement. We place visioning toward the end, not at the beginning, of the strategic planning process. We ask for key words and phrases that describe how your world will look different if you succeed in your strategic plan. Wordsmithing is not a large group activity. It is delegated to a small group.

Step Eight. Hold Yourself Accountable: Implement and Evaluate. After the plan is formally written and adopted, we emphasize quick movement toward implementation. Action steps need to include things to be done within the first three, six, nine, or twelve months. The plan becomes the focus for leaders, followers, and managers throughout the organization.

Our Strategic Planning Model

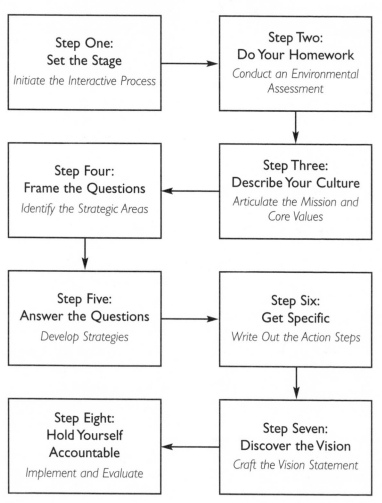

SET THE STAGE

Initiate the Interactive Process

"The beginning is the most important part of the work."

—Plato

The Davenport Fire Department needed a strategic plan. Stat.

Like virtually all of our clients, they had heard about us by word of mouth. They were impressed with the fact that we involved so many people in the planning process. They had heard that our interactive process built buy-in and increased the likelihood of implementation.

Their last plan was done several years ago with planners who specialize in working with firefighters. They had produced a long, glossy document with photos and testimonials, goals and objectives, timelines and benchmarks. It looked impressive. But for the most part, it had collected dust on a shelf. They wanted something different. We accepted their invitation and as usual, we scheduled the first meeting, which is intended to develop a plan to plan.

As we entered the fire station, it seemed we were walking into a time and place apart. The old firehouse had the look, feel, and smell of an old firehouse. Everything was fresh and polished. For over one hundred years, firefighters had protected the city from this location. We were hoping to preserve the tradition of courage, honor, and dedication lived out by the men and women who worked there. It was easy for us to share in their sense of mission. But we came with a lot of questions.

How could we make sure our plan did not suffer the same fate as the last one? How could we maximize the participation of the men and women who work so valiantly to protect our city? Who should be involved? In which steps?

This step will look at these questions. As we begin to explain our interactive planning process, we will start with the end in mind: How will the plan be implemented? We suggest that implementation is the key concern behind every decision made and every action taken in our first step: *setting the stage*.

PLANNING TO START

Setting the Stage is vital to most things. Strategic planning needs a script. You need to know who is going to do what and by when. You need to set the stage. Taking the time to set the stage may determine how well the other steps will proceed and whether the plan will be implemented.

Setting the stage means determining answers to the following questions:

- Who is going to be involved?
- How many people?
- What roles are they going to play?
- What is the timeline?
- What resources do we have?
- What are our planning assumptions?
- What are our planning mandates?
- Who are the decision makers?
- How will we gather the data to conduct the environmental assessment?

These questions need to be answered *before* the strategic planning process begins.

One factor that must be present from the outset is the unwavering commitment of those in authority. They will need to authorize resources for implementation. Getting a workforce energized about creating a strategic plan and then not following through will hurt morale. Strategic planning and implementation is the work of leaders *and* managers.

PLAN TO IMPLEMENT

A critical part of setting the stage is writing a script that looks *beyond* the end of the strategic planning process. Before we talk with clients about planning, timing, resources, or any other salient points about the process, we ask about implementation. If those in authority indicate a lack of interest in implementation, we stop right there.

We insist on an action plan that supports the strategic plan. In our process, people will be identified as responsible for each of the actions that will be taken. These individuals will need support from those in authority. Each action step is given a timeline and at the end of that period, the contact persons for that action item will be held accountable. The idea is to ensure that good intentions lead to good results. Once the strategic planning process is concluded, it is very easy for people to revert back to their day-to-day routines.

Follow-up meetings with the strategic planning team, board of directors, or whatever group is responsible for implementation must be held on a regular basis. We recommend quarterly meetings for follow-up reviews. Given a year to get things done, most people will wait and not begin work for several months, then have to scramble to take action at the last minute. Procrastination is the enemy of implementation.

Once the strategic planning sessions are completed, we set up accountability timelines at three, six, nine, and twelve months. That makes implementation more urgent right from the start. Three-month intervals generate enthusiasm for the plan and keep the process moving forward.

THE STRATEGIC PLANNING TEAM

Setting the stage also involves a thorough discussion of who will be involved and how. The more people you can involve, the more they will take ownership of the plan.

We have facilitated strategic planning processes involving as few as a handful of people and as many as fifty. We have involved as many as five hundred people in the early stages of the process. The number of people involved can depend on the size, diversity, and complexity of the organization. But one thing is clear: if the participation is limited to a select few, the process —and the resulting plan—will be owned by a select few.

The *strategic planning team* is the group of leaders, managers, members, and stakeholders who will participate in the strategic planning meetings that take the organization through the steps outlined in this book. In most cases, this involves two sessions that take about three to four hours each, depending on the size and complexity of the organization.

Usually, the first of these two planning sessions is *problem-seeking*. The result is identifying the key problems that will be addressed at the second meeting, which is *problem-solving*. That is when you come up with the strategies and action steps to address your problems.

The same team usually reconvenes for the quarterly accountability sessions held to evaluate the implementation of the plan.

MAXIMIZE PARTICIPATION

Exclusion is the enemy of ownership. Excluding certain people because you think they will be contrary is counterproductive. For example, we have encountered senior authorities who wanted to exclude union participation. They believed union reps would bog down the meeting by opposing anything new or innovative. Union members were seen as potentially disruptive, likely only to complain. These managers preferred to exclude unions from the process and tell them later what had been decided.

Let's think about this: Without being a part of the process, without being able to participate in the conversation, without having even a voice at the table, the union was expected to buy into the plan afterward. Is this realistic?

Inclusion is the path to ownership. We would much rather have stakeholder involvement—and that includes union participation—from the very beginning. Our goal is to engage as many stakeholders as possible throughout the process. Yes, the process may take a little longer, but it has been our experience that adoption of the plan will go more quickly and implementation of the plan will become more likely.

Dan was involved with a heating and air conditioning business called The Crawford Company. In 2011, the owners decided to involve all 72 of their employees in focus groups. This was intended to give voice to every employee in the organization.

Before the strategic planning meetings began, the owners had wanted to expand their facilities but didn't plan to start construction for at least three years. The focus group results changed their timetable. The employees stated clearly that the expansion needed to be done sooner rather than later. The focus group report gave the owners a greater sense of urgency about the need for capital improvements. In 2012, they built a 20,000 square foot expansion at a cost of $1.7 million. By 2013, the company had grown from

72 employees to 120. They enjoyed record growth and revenues in the process. It started with *choosing* to listen to their employees.[1]

For any organization, we suggest including a broad spectrum of stakeholders in the planning process. There are creative ways to involve large numbers of people. As the organization gets larger, you have to find ways to get smaller. We have many methods that involve small groups. One example is the core values process described in Step Three.

KEY STAKEHOLDERS

To set the stage, you have to identify the organization's stakeholders. We define a stakeholder as anyone who may be impacted by or care about the strategic plan. Armed with this definition, you can begin to understand the broad range of people your strategic planning process may affect.

Include a representative sample of organizational factions. We have worked with organizations too large to involve everyone in the focus groups beforehand. Instead, they held random selection processes to involve 10 to 20 percent of all employees with equitable inclusion of people from each division of the company. This is not optimal, but it is more realistic. It helps gain input from a representative variety of organizational members. That builds credibility and commitment when it comes to implementing the plan.

Fred facilitated the development of a strategic plan for the Davenport Junior Theater, the second oldest children's theater company in the country. In preliminary meetings with some of the theater's board members, they discussed involving community members, parents, and city officials. Then, one board member asked if Fred thought the children should be involved, which he was delighted to hear. Certainly, the children were the ultimate stakeholders.

There was some concern as to whether the children, especially the younger ones, would have enough of an attention span. Some board members thought they might become a distraction. After Fred showed his enthusiasm for the idea, they were added to the invitation list. It turned out to be one of the most enjoyable sessions Fred has ever facilitated, and the children added a lot to the process. After all, it was *their* theater company.

MANDATES

Setting the stage also includes the identification of mandates. *Mandates* identify issues that the organization *must* confront and ideas that are off limits. While we ask people to think "outside the box," we know that they also need to think "inside the circle" (see Figure 2).[2]

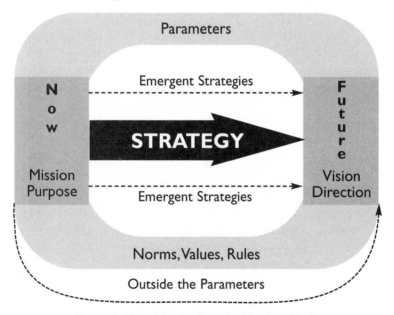

Figure 2: Outside the Box, Inside the Circle

The box around the word *strategy* in Figure 2 represents our intended strategy—that is, our usual way of thinking and acting. We want to think outside that box. The circle in Figure 2 represents the parameters around which you can think outside that box—that is, our mission, vision, values, rules, norms, and mandates. The space that is outside the box but inside the circle is fertile ground for new and creative strategies. The area outside the circle needs to be identified early in the strategic planning process.

Organizational mandates can help identify where you draw the circle. Mandates determine limits. They tell you what you must and must not deal with. Mandates are often set by outside entities such as accrediting bodies, governmental agencies, or higher levels of authority within the organization. There is no sense in chasing ideas that are dead on arrival because of a mandate.

Dan was facilitating strategic planning for an agency that involved the board in the first, but not the second, meeting of the strategic planning process. The CEO was trying to be careful not to overextend the time commitment of his board members. The idea was that the first meeting was to look more strategically at the organization, thus requiring input from the board. But the second meeting was focused on specific action steps that were going to be the responsibility of staff.

One group of staff came up with a very creative and ambitious idea for consolidation of all their offices into one location. The idea generated a lot of enthusiasm. The small work group working on that strategy came up with very specific steps to implement the idea. Yet, once they reported this idea back to the full group, the CEO pointed out that the idea had already been discussed and dismissed by the board. The employees were devastated. They never knew that consolidation was off-limits—an unstated mandate.

Two options could have prevented this misunderstanding:

1. Fully involve the board so they could speak to this idea directly; or
2. Exclude the idea of consolidation right from the start of the process.

Mandates can be as simple as dictating what the finished document should look like. They can be as major as mandating a no-new-hiring policy or requiring a balanced budget. They can establish process guidelines, timelines, resource allocations, or limits to what the team can consider.

Establishing these mandates sets the tone for the strategic planning process and defines just how creative the strategic planning team can get. It sets the parameters for decisions.

It is extremely important for those in positions of authority to let the team know the rules and boundaries very early in the process. This allows the team members to focus their efforts from the start.

On the other hand, too many mandates can stifle creativity. The more mandates that are put into place, the less creative the team can be. The tighter the circle of mandates, the less imaginative thinking can take place outside the box. Courageous leaders allow more room inside the circle so that people have more room to think outside the box.

CHANGE LAWS, RULES, OR MANDATES

Specific laws, rules, or mandates governing organizations can and should be identified at the beginning of the process. In addition, we suggest that the strategic planning team also consider the possibility that laws, rules, or mandates might be changed.

When a current law or mandate is too restrictive of the strategic planning process, it limits the team's creativity. Changing laws, rules, or mandates will most likely be difficult and may take a lot of time and energy, but sometimes, it can be done. If it is important for the organization's future well-being, you might want to try to change the rules that dictate your mandates.

Fred facilitated a strategic plan for a large organization that was attempting to bring multiple industrial facilities together into a single enterprise where members could work cohesively rather than competitively. These companies needed to operate out of the same set of business rules.

In order for that to happen, a law needed to be altered. As it turned out, the strategic planning process led to a discussion about changing that law. Discussions led to action and eventually, a major law impacting the industrial facilities was indeed changed. In fact, it was a direct result of the creative thinking that occurred during the strategic planning process.

Some mandates can be internally driven—created by the organization itself. They might be policies and procedures set by the board or management team. While we understand the need for some mandates, we caution those in authority to use them judiciously. The more mandates you put in place, the less creative the strategic planning team can be.

Empower your people to be as creative as possible from the start. Let them formulate ideas without too much constraint. Let them brainstorm ideas that have few boundaries. Allow leeway for those implementing the plan as to how they will do that job—as long as it fits into the overall strategy.

You might be surprised at the ideas people come up with and the innovative ways they devise to implement them. Strategic planning recommendations can always be pared back later. To inhibit the thought process upfront is to inhibit the process in general.

USE OF A FACILITATOR

A *facilitator* is someone who pays particular attention to the process itself and makes sure it keeps moving. It is quite normal for discussions to bog down when people get into the "weeds," which is to say small, immaterial, and/or controversial details. While such a discussion can occasionally be valuable, too much of it will stymie the process.

Inside facilitators are people who work inside the organization. They know the organization well. They know the language and can fully understand the nuances of the discussions. That familiarity can also be a disadvantage. The temptation is to participate instead of facilitate. We have found from personal experience that it is impractical to participate *and* to facilitate at the same time. The facilitation role will suffer.

A lack of objectivity can make it hard for inside facilitators to check their emotions or to avoid influencing the discussion to suit their opinions and preferences. This can create conflict within the organization and short-circuit the process. Whether the intention is to manipulate the results or not, it can appear that way to other participants.

Another potential drawback of inside facilitators is their preexisting relationships. Their relationships with bosses, coworkers, and certain departments can affect how they maintain equitable participation between the quick talkers and the quiet participants. It can also limit the response they get from certain participants due to prior experiences.

Inside facilitators can also suffer from thinking, "We tried that before and it doesn't work." All facilitators need to open up the group to creative thinking without suffering from restrictions or biases about what might work and what has already been tried.

We have seen plenty of organizations try to conduct strategic planning with facilitation by a senior authority, top manager, or board member of that organization. In fact, we have been in that position of facilitating as insiders ourselves. What we have discovered is that trying to fulfill both roles simply does not work.

At one moment, you might be facilitating well, and then something is shared and you feel a strong need to address the substance of that issue. Once you speak to that issue, you are no longer facilitating. In fact, we have discovered that inside facilitators often are caught up in the subject matter and need to be facilitated themselves. It is very easy—and sometimes tempting—to use the role of facilitator to manipulate the decisions being made.

In most cases, we believe it is best to utilize an *outside facilitator*. In our experience, an independent, objective person brings significant value to the process. The outside facilitator can lead the process without having to worry about interoffice repercussions, ongoing relationships, or competing values. The outside facilitator can ask hard questions, challenge thinking, stop non-value-added conversations, keep things on time, make sure everyone is participating, and perform a host of other facilitator roles more freely.

It is particularly important to note that outside facilitators *do not* make strategic decisions. Instead, they

- Create a positive planning environment;
- Structure the strategic planning process;
- Facilitate the group interaction in order to enhance participation;
- Keep the group focused on the task at hand;
- Encourage the group to think strategically;
- Stimulate conflict around the problem without getting personal;
- Move the process forward in a positive direction and a timely manner; and
- Consult with one or two people who will write the strategic plan.

When we facilitate, we share examples of strategic plans, mission statements, strategic areas, strategies, action steps, core values statements, and vision statements with those writing the plan, and provide online feedback on the various drafts of each of these parts of the plan.[3]

CONCLUSION

Working with the Davenport Fire Department, we found ways of recruiting the right mix of people and involving as many people as possible—thereby expanding the sense of ownership. In fact, we included about fifty people on the strategic planning team: the department's management team, many of the firefighters themselves, community leaders and partners, elected officials, city staff, and other first responders from the local community.[4]

Setting the stage sets the tone for the entire strategic planning process. It is essential that everyone involved understands his or her role in the process. Taking the time to set the stage saves time, builds trust, and lays the foundation for a smooth process. It is important to clarify right at the beginning why the strategic plan is being developed, how it will be implemented, and what is expected of everyone on the strategic planning team.

We find differing points of view to be of value—before, during, and after the strategic planning sessions. Inclusion gives people an opportunity to contribute perspectives and ideas that enhance the process. You discover opportunities you might have missed. As was the case with the firefighters, it generates more interesting conversations and gives a larger number of people a sense of ownership in the eventual plan.

DO YOUR HOMEWORK

Conduct an Environmental Assessment

"Give me six hours to chop down a tree and I will spend the first four sharpening the axe."
—Abraham Lincoln

Meeting in that old fire station, the strategic planning team was eager to get started. The leaders and managers of the fire department had waited long enough. They were ready to clear their calendars and get down to business. As we discussed our interactive planning process, they got excited about our suggestions for the next step in the process: *doing your homework.*

They had decided to hold two planning sessions and to invite about fifty people to participate as members of the strategic planning team. The first session would include our core values process, a SWOT analysis (Strengths, Weaknesses, Opportunities, and Threats), and the identification of three strategic areas. At the second session, we would develop strategies and action steps for each strategic area. We would conclude with our short visioning process.

At our suggestion, they realized that they could also gain the input of additional people by holding focus group meetings. As a result, they asked us to facilitate five internal focus groups to listen to as many members of their union as possible, and five external focus groups to dialogue with leaders, partners, and members of the community.

Focus groups are just one of the research methods we will discuss in this step. They are a very participative method used to gain insight from a variety of voices who will not necessarily be involved on the strategic planning team.

The conventional wisdom says you start at the beginning. After our initial contact with a new client, most people are eager to begin their strategic planning session right away. However, *before* you sit down to plan strategically, you need to do your homework. It is critical that the whole strategic planning team takes time to prepare before they meet for the first planning session.

CONSIDER YOUR FRAMES

Frames are the windows through which you view the world. They are the lens you use to focus on what you see and what you know. Frames can become *biases* because they invite planners to prejudge information too quickly. Frames can enhance or diminish certain pieces of data, depending on whether the data fits your personal preferences.

When you frame a picture, you can literally decide which part of the picture is in or out. You can cut and paste what you want to see. You can set the limits to what you see and what you don't see. Frames can be expanding or limiting, depending on how open you are to seeing the whole world. You can invite new perspectives or ignore them.

Going into a strategic planning process with information co-opted by personal biases can sabotage the process from the very start. It is critical that strategic planners understand their biases and take steps to overcome them. Planners must identify their biases, look beyond them, expand their frames, and seek and seriously consider the assessments of others.

To plan strategically, you first must intentionally, diligently, and aggressively challenge your personal frames, biases, and assumptions.

HINDSIGHT, INSIGHT, AND FORESIGHT

As a leader, you need hindsight, insight, and foresight about strategy. You need hindsight into the past, insight into what is happening now, and foresight about what will be happening next in the marketplace of your business.

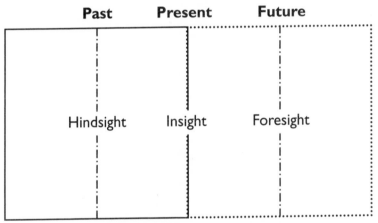

Figure 3: Each step in our process requires
hindsight, insight, and foresight.

Insight begins with an honest reflection on hindsight. Hindsight is not always twenty-twenty. You need reflection on your experiences for that hindsight to become clear. Wisdom is knowledge based on experience. Some people grow in wisdom from difficult experiences. Others do not. Wisdom emerges out of reflection about experiences. Wisdom nurtures hindsight into the past and insight into the present to nurture foresight about the future.

Strategic leaders need foresight to identify future trends. Foresight is the ability to see what is coming next. It is not so much a trait as a skill that can be developed by careful research, personal reflection, and interactive discussion about the signs of the times. When reading books, articles, and the news each day, ask yourself what trends will impact your business the most in the next three to five years. Remain open to the ideas of others, especially those who disagree with you.

Strategic leaders see the whole landscape. As a strategic leader, you must "get on the balcony" and look objectively at your organization, your business, your colleagues, and yourself, as if everyone was on a stage and you were watching the action from a balcony.[1] This can provide you with hindsight about the past, insight into the present, and foresight for the future.

GATHER THE DATA

The next step is gathering the data that can be useful for intelligence. This is not the same as gathering *information*. The relevant information that will be used for decision-making is called *intelligence*.[2]

Data needs to be gathered both inside and outside the organization. The data you gather must be relevant to the strategic planning process. It must provide hindsight into the past, insight into the present, and foresight about the future.

The key to gathering the intelligence is to *listen* to all perspectives. Strategic planners need to go out of their way to hear from any stakeholders with an opposite viewpoint. Avoid the temptation to gather intelligence only from the sources that confirm your preconceived biases. Listen to the naysayers. Seek out sources that will challenge your comfort level.

Some planners ignore this kind of homework. They are limited by their frames. Some think that looking beyond their personal frames is a waste of time. Or they may simply want to control the results—regardless of the facts.

The key is to identify what new perspective each individual group can offer. A small midwestern city began its intelligence gathering by meeting first with owners of two large businesses located within its borders. The city manager and facilitator met next with a group of five small business owners. That was followed by a session with municipal board members and civic volunteers. Finally, a group consisting of neighborhood activists and local educators was convened.

It was a good start. But the planners purposefully excluded two key groups of stakeholders—unionized city employees and taxpayers. They were afraid that both would come armed with complaints and criticism that city officials did not want to hear. This left a major gap in the collection of the intelligence.

If you have not gathered intelligence that disagrees with your personal frame, or gives you cause for discomfort, go back and get it. Make yourself uncomfortable.

PERFORM A LITERATURE SEARCH

A literature search can help you gather intelligence from business journals, trade publications, even newspaper and magazine stories. Any source that has anything to do with your business can be reviewed for intelligence. This is particularly true for literature sources that analyze your business for emerging themes and trends.

Fred worked for a senior authority who wanted to develop a strategic direction in only three days. The senior authority called in several critical stakeholders from around the country for a quick, two-day strategic planning meeting. Fred asked each of the stakeholders to conduct a literature search beforehand and to arrive prepared to give a summary of the literature they discovered.

Some of what these stakeholders found was expected. Predictable. Other intelligence was unanticipated. The group was inclined to dismiss the unanticipated and unwanted intelligence. Fred encouraged them to consider all of it. The unexpected intelligence identified several important trends and potentially significant threats on the organizational horizon. In the end, the group decided to use this information and thus was able to develop a thorough, realistic strategic direction.

BRING IN A GUEST SPEAKER

Intelligence also can be found in expert testimony. We encourage organizations to invite experts in a particular business or trade to speak to the strategic planning team *before* the first session. Team-wide interaction with an expert can spark productive conversation in advance of strategic planning. It can particularly help stimulate thinking about major trends in your business.

For example, Dan was facilitating strategic planning for a symphony orchestra that invited a guest speaker from a national association in New York. The night before the strategic planning session, the expert spoke at a dinner for the board, staff, and musicians who were on the strategic planning team. He showed data suggesting trends in small-to-medium sized orchestras around the country. His presentation stirred new conversations about some disturbing trends and some exciting opportunities.

CONDUCT A SURVEY

Surveys provide a more complete and structured way to gather information.[3] They offer an easy way to gather intelligence from both internal and external sources. With online resources today, surveys can be distributed and collected easily.

The key is to develop a high-quality survey that will provide participants opportunities to respond fully *and* freely. A well-executed survey will encourage honest feedback. Designing a survey to protect strategic planners and organizations from criticism renders the survey useless from the start. You want to receive the criticism so that you can take assertive action to fix problems. Be careful to prevent internal bias in your survey.

HOLD FOCUS GROUPS

Focus groups are a great way to expand stakeholder participation. The process begins with identifying groups of stakeholders by categories, such as affiliated departments, management, unions, and so on. External groups can include clients, business owners, community partners, special interest groups, or any group that can add to the intelligence.

Advantages and Limitations of Focus Groups. The interaction of a focus group session can stimulate new ideas that one person filling out a survey does not. The focus group creates a laboratory for creative ideas. One idea leads to a better idea, and a better idea leads to the best idea. For this level of synergy to occur, facilitation has to generate effective interaction and full participation.

That being said, even the best facilitation cannot overcome the reluctance that some people might have to speak out if they do not trust the other participants in the room. When conducting internal focus groups, it is particularly important for the facilitator to pay attention to this limitation. It can become a particular issue when any participant is in a focus group with his or her immediate supervisor—a situation we try to avoid whenever possible.

As a qualitative source of data, focus groups do not provide a statistical picture of how many people agree or disagree with certain ideas or viewpoints. However, they do provide a rich source of inputs that are not readily available in any other way.[4]

When we conduct focus groups as part of a strategic planning session, we usually schedule sessions with a variety of constituencies. For example, before developing a plan for Scott County, Iowa, we convened each of the county's sixteen departments as a focus group. A summary focus group report identified the specific priorities of each department.

When focus groups involve a mix of constituencies, the summary report is less valuable because facilitators cannot distinguish the feedback between one group of stakeholders and another. This limitation must be noted in the summary report.

The Focus Group Interview Guide. In a focus group, the group meeting itself is the research instrument. The *focus group interview guide* is carefully designed by the facilitator in consultation with the interested organization. The usual set of general questions that we ask is included in Figure 4. These are designed around a traditional SWOT analysis.

We ask the organization if they have any *focused questions* to be added to our usual list of questions. Focused questions are those added specifically at the request of the organization being studied. Examples include questions about a new initiative the organization has launched, a new opportunity on their horizon, or a new challenge they are facing. Questions on these topics can be added to the list of questions being asked. Or they can be asked by the facilitator *only if* the subject does not come up by itself. In fact, one of the focus group results can be whether the topic came up spontaneously or whether the facilitators had to ask the question first.

Sometimes what is *not* said in a focus group is more important than what *is* said. Dan was conducting a round of focus groups for The Crawford Company when their founder, Bob Frink, was moving into partial retirement. Concern about the

---

Our Focus Interview Guide

1. What are your general impressions about this organization?

2. What are the strengths of the organization?

3. What are the weaknesses of the organization?

4. What are some improvements that can be made to the organization?

5. What should the organization stop doing (if anything)?

6. Where are opportunities for growth?

7. What threats are there to the organization?

8. List strategies for moving forward.

9. Final thoughts or comments.

Figure 4: Focus Group Interview Guide

future at the top of the company was a major finding of those focus groups. Employees were feeling nervous about Bob's retirement and were somewhat reluctant to talk about it.

One year later, when The Crawford Company asked Dan to conduct another round of focus groups, the topic of Bob's retirement did not come up. Not even once. The younger owners of the company had obviously stepped up in Bob's absence. People felt confident in the new leadership. In fact, after Dan issued the focus group report and held a meeting with the owners, the first thing Bob said about the report was, "I was so relieved to see that my retirement was not mentioned in the report."

If Dan had asked people about Bob's retirement, the focus group would not have determined this important result. This is why it is important for the facilitator of a focus group not to insert his or her own bias by asking specific questions about matters that are not first presented by the participants. Once a subject comes up, the facilitator can probe more deeply to clarify that concern. But if a subject has not come up, and the organization has not asked the facilitator to ask specifically about that subject matter, it is a mistake to ask leading questions about that topic.

Facilitation. Some of our best lessons emerge from our worst experiences. We can all relate to the frustration of being in meetings where the facilitators allow one or two people to dominate. Most participants in a meeting of any type appreciate facilitation. Some people will speak out at every opportunity at every meeting they attend. Often it is a person who likes to be in control, a dominant member of the group. Sometimes it is a person who is just uncomfortable with silence. Others are just wired to be talkers.

Whatever the reason, some participants will need to be controlled—sometimes even interrupted—for the sake of the rest of the group and the success of the meeting.

The focus group facilitator needs to discourage the dominant behavior of the few and encourage the quiet participants to open up. Sometimes doing the latter accomplishes the former. By calling on the quiet participants, the facilitator can sometimes redirect the domineering behavior of those who talk too much. At other times, the facilitator may have to be more direct and ask the loud participants to give others a chance to talk.

We have facilitated literally hundreds of focus groups in preparation for strategic planning. The biggest lesson we have learned about facilitation is to *listen*. Yes, to listen. Then to summarize, very briefly, what a participant has said.

Summarization is an art. It is sometimes necessary to check with the speaker to make sure that the paraphrasing is accurate. Reflecting emotions can be necessary as well. For example, someone in a focus group might be expressing some frustration. Reflecting that emotion goes simply like this: "That sounds really frustrating." Reflecting emotions allows the speaker to vent. Reflecting and summarizing are key to good facilitation.[5]

SCHEDULE INTERVIEWS

One-on-one interviews are another way of gathering intelligence before a strategic planning process. Such interviews can follow the same list of nine questions that we use in focus groups, as well as any focused questions that the organization wants to add.

The most important skill for these interviews is to listen. Summarize ideas and give the other person a chance to respond to the summary to ensure accuracy.

Dan once interviewed the CEO of a hospital whose grasp of the complexities of health care reform was impressive. He had a remarkable ability to express complex ideas in such a way as to make health care reform sound simple. In the process of Dan's summary of the interviewee's responses, the CEO stopped him to remark, "You sure know a lot about health care." Dan responded, "Well, thanks just the same, but I'm just learning all of this from you." Clearly, the summary was on target.

The biggest mistake a facilitator can make is talking too much. The primary role of the facilitator is to listen and summarize, not to make his or her own contributions. We also find that facilitation requires the ability to pause and allow for some quiet space after a good question is asked, instead of rushing to fill that silence with another comment or question.

CALL FOR A STRATEGIC ASSESSMENT

A strategic assessment is an extensive search for data by experts using all the information gathering techniques already described in this step. It is an unfiltered, empirical analysis of the intelligence, usually from an outside expert (or group of experts). Strategic assessments can be costly but are a considerably more thorough and usually less biased analysis of the data.

During the late 1980s, Fred worked for an organization that managed maintenance and supply installations for the military. Most of these facilities were built during World War II, and the organization was looking into a large modernization program that could cost over $1 billion.

Fred quickly discovered there was no readily available information as to what the future might hold for these installations. He recommended a strategic assessment. An independent contractor was hired to conduct several hundred interviews of experts in the field, that is, executives from the Department of the Army, the Department of Defense, and the defense industry. Their assessment of the situation painted a clear picture of what the future would very likely hold for the supply and maintenance installations. And it was nothing like the existing environment.

The strategic assessment identified a future that seemed radical in that moment, but which soon became a reality when the Berlin Wall fell and defense spending was cut. The assessment led to the timely implementation of strategies and actions others in the industry were very slow to take.

PROCESS CHECK

Once the data has been gathered, ask yourself the following questions:

- What are the themes that emerge from the data?
- How can we translate that data into intelligence?
- What parts of the data will be most valuable during the strategic planning sessions?

Assessing the myriad of gathered intelligence and synthesizing it for further use is the homework that needs to be done by the strategic planning team in order to prepare for Step Four of our process: *identifying the strategic areas*.

However, before entering further into the discussion about using the intelligence, we will insert another important aspect of strategic planning: *articulating the mission and core values*.

CONCLUSION

Gathering data through the ten focus groups held by the Davenport Fire Department was a critical step in the strategic planning process. The focus group report we submitted provided valuable input. It gave the fifty members of the strategic planning team a lot to think about. More people involved meant more ideas to consider. It also extended the sense of participation to about one hundred more people involved in the focus groups.

Before the first strategic planning session is held, the strategic planning team can conduct an environmental assessment by doing literature searches, conducting interviews and focus groups, and maybe even hiring out a strategic assessment. Whatever research method is employed, it is critical that the strategic planning team does its homework so it can make informed decisions.

Data gathered in this process—whether it fits your frames or not—must be translated into intelligence needed for strategic planning. You need hindsight about the past, insight into the present, and foresight about the future to convert your data into intelligence.

DESCRIBE YOUR CULTURE

Articulate the Mission and Core Values

"It's not hard to make decisions when you know what your values are."

—Roy Disney

Max was a blue-collar worker. A strong, tough, and rugged sort of guy. He was a paramedic for Medic EMS, an organization going into our strategic planning process.[1] Everyone in the room seemed surprised when Max talked about his core value: *compassion.* He said that being compassionate about the people in his rig—the patients and his coworkers, the people he rode alongside—was his number one priority. It personified everything he did.

Sam got up to speak. He said that being *professional* was his number one core value. He said that the uniform he wears has special meaning. The name on his uniform speaks volumes. It means everything to him. It represents an unwavering commitment to excellence. It means being professional in all he says and does.

The board and staff at Medic EMS had asked Dan to organize a core values process. The CEO had sent out a notice requiring every employee to attend a core values meeting. At first, many of them seemed uncomfortable being there; they wondered, "What does this have to do with strategic planning?" Some struggled with the concept of core values.

But the process gave them a structured way to talk about what was important to them. Once they got up and started speaking about how and why they worked as paramedics, they were fully engaged.

Some of the most moving moments in strategic planning can occur when members of the organization get up and speak about what means the most to them: their mission and core values. We believe that the first strategic planning session should start by identifying, strengthening, and building greater commitment to the philosophy of the organization, that is, its mission and values. In fact, this philosophy should drive the strategic planning process.

ORGANIZATIONAL CULTURE

The culture of an organization surrounds us like the air we breathe. It can impact everything we think, say, and do. Culture is how we say, do, and interpret things within an organization. Culture is depicted by the organization's statements, plans, and behaviors. It is expressed in core values, philosophy, and beliefs.[2]

Your organization has a culture, whether you know it or not. Strategic planning provides an opportunity to focus more intentionally on that culture. A good strategic plan includes statements of mission, vision, and values. If written well, mission and values statements rarely need to be changed—perhaps every ten to fifteen years. (In the case of vision statements, which are addressed in Step Seven, they can be updated more often.) The strategic planning process is a time to reflect on mission and core values.

MISSION

The core of mission is *purpose*. A mission statement has three components: (1) business, (2) purpose, and (3) values. The *business* of an organization is what it does, that is, the products or services it provides.[3] Business is usually more concrete, specific, and easy to identify.

Purpose adds social benefit to society—that is, to the people, community, or communities served by an organization. Identifying and articulating the purpose of an organization can be difficult. A common mistake is to confuse business with purpose.

- *Planting trees and flowers* might be your business (what you do).
- *To beautify the neighborhood* might be your purpose (why you do it).
- Put together, you might say:
  - *To beautify the neighborhood by planting trees and flowers.*

Purpose brings substance to a strategic plan. Purpose appeals to those outside the organization and provides meaning to people within it. Purpose suggests ways that the day-to-day work inside an organization contributes to something greater, to the greater good beyond its walls.

Some people assume that only not-for-profit and public organizations need to appeal to a sense of purpose. We believe this is a mistake, a missed opportunity. In fact, for-profit corporations also have a lot to gain by asking themselves what social benefit they are providing to their communities. And by this, we don't mean only the financial contributions the company makes to United Way or the volunteer work that employees perform for Habitat for Humanity.

The business of any company should provide some type of benefit to society. Construction companies make our roads safer. Agricultural firms help to feed the world. Financial planners enhance family security. Most companies are not only building a product or providing a service (their business) but are meeting a basic human need (their purpose).

All three sectors of organizational society—for-profit, not-for-profit, and public institutions—can benefit from appealing to a sense of purpose. Mission is more fundamental than even the financial bottom line. Leaders who figure this out, and live this out with credibility, become even more successful. Mission and money can have a reciprocal effect on each other: The more your organization can appeal to mission, the more profitable you can become. And the more profitable you become, the more mission you can accomplish.[4] This is true for *all* organizations: publics, for-profits, and not-for-profits. The not-for-profit organization simply reinvests the "profit" into more mission.

TRANSFORMATIONAL LEADERSHIP

Appealing to mission is one way to intrinsically motivate employees.[5] This means the people are internally driven to engage in the work more willingly. It provides *inspirational motivation*. It is one of the four major components to transformational leadership. Igniting a sense of purpose can inspire people inside the organization to work beyond minimum performance levels. It can promote dignity and enhance meaning in their work.

Consider this story: Three men are building a wall when a passerby asks them what they are doing. The first man says, "Can't you see, I'm laying bricks." The second person says, "I'm building a wall." And the third one answers, "I'm building a cathedral." Of the three men, which one has a greater sense of purpose? Which one will be more motivated? Knowing that you are building a cathedral should enhance motivation.

Purpose helps people see how their small part fits into a whole picture and how what they do every day benefits society in some way. This can help motivate members of an organization to perform *organizational citizenship behaviors*.[6] These are simple behaviors associated with transformational leadership and with teams that are performing at a high level.

Many of us are looking for ways to give meaning and purpose to our lives. We spend forty-plus hours per week at work and would like to know that we are contributing something to the greater good in the process. By appealing to organizational purpose, leaders can bring meaning to that forty-hour workweek. The valuable result is more *intrinsic motivation*.

MISSION STATEMENTS

It is our belief that mission statements should be just that—*statements*. They should be clear and concise, simple and to the point. They should briefly state what the organization does and why. If a mission statement is too wordy, it will go unnoticed, unread, and unappreciated. It is far too valuable to allow that to happen.

A mission statement should be memorable and memorizable. It should focus on the present, not the future. The vision statement will focus on the future (see Step Seven).

Writing a mission statement requires looking at your business, purpose, and values, then editing the results to form a concise, clear statement.

1. *Business*. Focus first on your business. This is the phrase of your mission statement that often begins with the words "by providing." Once you know what you provide (that's the easy part), it makes it clearer that the next step must go deeper.

    For example, a homeless shelter "provides emergency and transitional shelter," a restaurant "provides a wide variety of Italian dishes," and a public school system "provides educational opportunities for children of all ages."

2. *Purpose.* Identify the social purpose your business can and does fulfill. This can be the toughest challenge because few of us think about our purpose. To identify social purpose, we need to focus on our customers, clients, or the people we serve—that is, the community and society in general. What difference is our business making to others? What fundamental human need is met through our work?

The homeless shelter might say that it "builds hope for the homeless by providing emergency and transitional shelter." The restaurant might say it "takes our diners to the heart of Italy by providing a wide variety of Italian dishes." The school system "prepares future generations for a global world by providing educational opportunities for children of all ages."

3. *Values.* Add a phrase about your core values. The core values aspect of the mission statement adds colorful expression and serves to modify and amplify the statement's purpose and business elements. The words you select are usually similar to, but not necessarily the same as, the core values you select in the core values process we describe below.

The homeless shelter builds hope for the homeless by providing *dignified* emergency and transitional shelter. The restaurant might add that it provides a wide variety of *exquisite* Italian dishes. The school system prepares future generations for a global world by providing educational opportunities that will *challenge* children of all ages.

4. *Editing.* Once you have the mission statement crafted, look to see how you can reduce its length. The last step in drafting a mission statement is to ask if every word and phrase is absolutely necessary. Try some creative writing. See if you can eliminate the phrase, "by providing."

With some creativity, you might discover a phrase that can capture the essence of business *and* purpose. For example, a small liberal arts college might say their mission is *"preparing students for life's journey."* This could be their business (what they do) and their purpose (why they do it). In this case, the purpose of the college would be succinct and obvious. This mission statement would also suggest that the college is *student-centered* (a core value).

CORE VALUES

Strategic planning presents an organization with the opportunity to identify, articulate, and build commitment to core values, which in turn should drive any decision-making process for that organization. They are the core beliefs, the philosophy of the organization. Once an organization is clear about its core values, decision making becomes much easier. Core values can become the simple rules that govern programs, policies, and procedures. They inform and impact all decisions.

For example, core values can be used for hiring decisions. Many organizations make the mistake of hiring people whose core values might conflict with the *values* held by the company because they have the right *skills* needed for a position. If our core values are impacting our decision making, we should test candidates not only for their skills but for their values. In many cases, it is easier to improve a practical skill than to change core values after someone is hired.

When interviewing for new employees, we suggest that you design interview questions that explore the core values of a candidate. For example, if the company values safety over speed, then design interview questions to test whether the candidates' views are aligned with the core value of safety.

Once you know your core values, you can design questions around real-life situations and ask the interviewees how they would handle those situations. Think in advance about several ways that each question might be answered and assign scores to each possible answer. Your core values will help you measure each candidate if you determine the best answers.

Expressive and Instrumental Values. Core values can be instrumental (the how) and expressive (the why). *Instrumental values* describe the business of the organization—how things are done—such as collaboration, teamwork, and quality. *Expressive values* explain the purpose of the organization, such as social justice, public health, and quality of life.

Expressive values are the ends (the results we have in mind). Instrumental values are the means (the way we get there). As we stated earlier, a mission statement needs to address business and purpose. Similarly, the core values used in the mission and core values statements should incorporate both the instrumental and expressive sides of the equation.

Dan was working with the board of the Friends of Vander Veer Park, a volunteer group that provides support for a neighborhood park. Initially, the board identified core values like *collaborative*, *resourceful*, and *creative*. These are instrumental values because they suggest how the Friends group operates. Dan probed deeper about why the organization exists. At first, the group members suggested *quality of life*. Dan asked what aspects of quality of life the organization fulfills. Eventually, the board members expressed the values of *recreation* and *beauty*, which express two of the core reasons the group exists.

Adding the expressive values to the instrumental values gives a more complete picture of the *philosophy* of the organization. Putting all the pieces together, the mission statement of the Friends of Vander Veer Park reads as follows: *"We work collaboratively, creatively, and resourcefully to enhance the quality of life of the neighborhood with opportunities for beauty and recreation."*

CORE VALUES STATEMENTS

We believe that discussing mission and core values sets the tone for strategic planning. It reminds people of the organization's essential reason for being. Values focus on the culture and philosophy of the organization. By focusing on these early in the strategic planning process, we ground our discussions in that culture and philosophy.

Our core values process is interactive, fun, and meaningful. It not only helps an organization to identify its core values, it also increases commitment to those values. The product is a *core values statement*. But the process itself can be more valuable because it raises the commitment to those values by all participants—employees, owners, administrators, and all stakeholders involved. Focusing on core values is a powerful exercise. Just discussing core values can have a major impact on people.

Dan has used the core values process with over fifty organizations, involving hundreds of people in some cases. He first developed the process working with John Kiley, a friend who at the time was CEO at United Way of the Quad Cities. Together, Dan and John used the process with the staff, the board, and all the agency directors of United Way. The resulting statement was adopted by the board, advertised in all United Way materials, and used in decision making.

Working with the Girl Scouts of Eastern Iowa and Western Illinois, Dan involved four hundred parents, leaders, and girl scouts in the core values process.[7] The most powerful part of that experience was hearing the girls get up in front of large audiences and articulate the values of *service, character, empowerment,* and *relationships.* The final writing process, which involved several of the girls themselves, included a long discussion about the meaning of the value *relationships,* which was eventually defined: *"We provide a fun and accepting environment to build friendships and develop partnerships."*

THE CORE VALUES PROCESS

The core values process can be conducted through a series of meetings held in advance of the strategic planning sessions. We have run this core values process with *all* employees of many health care organizations, public agencies, social service providers, and a heating and air conditioning business. Typically, employees are required to attend one session, sometimes during regular hours, sometimes during lunch hours or at shift changes.

Here are the steps to our core values process:

1. *Individual Reflection.* Read through the provided list of core values.[8] Circle those core values that resonate when you think of your organization: What does your organization believe in? Identify those values that you already practice. You don't want to preach values you don't practice. This creates a credibility gap. Think of values not on the list that fit your organization. Add these on the blank lines. Then list your top five values.

2. *One-on-Ones.* Find a "shoulder partner" (someone near your shoulder). Working with that person,

come to a consensus about your top five values. Remember, it is not your personal values you are identifying. It is the values of your organization. Talk about what these values mean in your own words and discuss how they are practiced. Be careful not to use any quantitative methods, such as quid pro quos, to make your decision. Try to persuade each other. When you reach an agreement, write your top five values on the large charts posted on the walls. Put both names next to your list.

3. *Speak Out.* This is the most powerful step in the process. Working with your partner, get up and tell the rest of the group in your own words what these values mean to you and to your organization. Speak from the heart. Talk about specific ways that the organization practices these values. Make sure you have someone taking careful notes during this step to record the words associated with each of the values discussed.

4. *Decide.* Make a master list of any core values that were included in the previous step. Working individually, vote for five of the core values on this list. Be open to the possibility of changing your mind based on how others have talked about these core values. Try to include a good mix of instrumental values (describing the business) and expressive values (explaining the purpose). When the core values process is part of strategic planning, we usually have people do the voting on these values during a break in the action.[9]

5. *Write Your Statement.* Use your best judgment to find five to seven core values that received the most support. Find two or three volunteers who

seem very engaged in this process to work with the facilitators and transform these results into a core values statement. Circulate the notes from this process along with sample core values statements. Ask one volunteer to write the first draft and circulate it to the facilitators and other volunteers for feedback and input. Develop a draft of the core values statement and present it later to those authorized to approve it.

Remember, the goal of this activity is not to *change* the culture but to *articulate* it. If we preach a core value that we are not practicing, we create a credibility gap. For example, if an organization states that it is family-friendly but does not practice that value, it has created an even bigger problem. If the culture needs to change, the best approach is to write behavioral changes into the strategies of your strategic plan. The culture of an organization will change when the attitudes and behaviors of the people change first.

We have often been very moved by this core values process. Listening to paramedics, plumbers, social workers and kids, board members and staff, carpenters, nurses, and engineers talking about core values can be a powerful experience.

Feedback from participants in our core values process has always been very positive. We regularly hear participants describe the experience with words such as "inspiring...uplifting... engaging...a lot of fun."

The core values process has *two outcomes*:

1. *Process*—talking about core values builds *commitment* to those values.
2. *Product*—writing up the results produces a *core values statement*.

MISSION AND THE CORE VALUES PROCESS

If your organization already has a mission statement before entering into the strategic planning process, we use the core values process as a participative way to engage the strategic planning team in discussions about that mission—and possibly to update the wording. The core values process can help you clarify your mission because the core values can be distinguished by instrumental (business) and expressive (purpose) values.

The core values process also helps distinguish which values might be incorporated into the mission statement and which ones are better suited for the core values statement. We prefer not to clutter the mission statement with too many core values— especially not the instrumental values. Expressive values are a better fit because they articulate a sense of purpose. Instead, the core values statement can be a corollary statement, one that is marketed right along with the mission statement—and eventually the vision statement (see Step Seven).

MARKETING AND COMMUNICATION

We have seen many creative uses of these statements. Most organizations put them on their websites. Family Resources Inc. created a beautiful, one-page flyer and poster with their mission, vision, and values statements.[10] They framed the poster and placed it around their campus. The Crawford Company painted it on the walls in both of their conference rooms.

Almost everyone who has been involved in this process agrees that the most valuable outcome is the commitment it builds for the core values themselves. It gets everyone on the same page and creates excitement. We get very positive feedback about the process itself.

CONCLUSION

When Max and Sam got up to speak about compassion and professionalism, they were identifying a starting point for the strategic planning process for Medic EMS. Strategic decisions ought to be made in the context of mission and core values. Whatever Medic decided to do strategically, it had to be consistent with and driven by mission.

Strategic planning provides an opportunity for leaders to reflect upon culture. Leaders cultivate the mission, vision, and values of a company. They create statements to articulate mission, vision, and values. By involving many stakeholders in our interactive processes, leaders build commitment, develop interest, and frame the activities of the organization around mission, vision, and values.

The statements produced during strategic planning can provide a basis for continuous focus on the culture of the organization. Leaders hire, excite, and continuously realign their people based on mission, vision, and values. Ultimately, leaders create a new culture. But that is the last step in leading change. Leaders initiate a discussion to identify, articulate, and build commitment to culture and all of its elements.

FRAME THE QUESTIONS

Identify the Strategic Areas

"If you can get a clear picture of your goal, really see
it, feel it, taste it, then you can make it happen."
—Arlene Blum

LMX Engineering had a lot of conflicting voices and too many
priority issues. The leaders and managers came to the strategic
planning process with a long list of ideas. Plenty of new places
to go. New things to do. But not enough people to do them.

Each issue brought its own sense of urgency and importance. Each one needed to be addressed—immediately. Everything seemed like a major priority.

The easy answer was to place each of these items on the
agenda and make sure all the bases were covered. After all, that
would make everyone happy. It would be the path of least resistance. Eventually, LMX might get around to meeting all these
needs and issues.

We can remember the days when strategic planning meant
answering all the issues facing an organization. That is not the
way we conduct strategic planning today.

We are sometimes asked what step in our process is prioritization. The answer is every step, not just this one. But it is particularly important to this next step: *framing the questions*.

After the homework has been done and the mission and values have been articulated, the strategic planning team is ready to get into strategy. At that first meeting, the adrenaline is flowing. The energy level is high. And at this point, the greatest temptation is to try to do too much. If that happens, implementation of the strategic plan can become unrealistic.

CHALLENGING BUT NOT OVERWHELMING

Imagine: if you have 5 strategic areas in your strategic plan and 5 strategies per strategic area and 5 action steps per strategy, that would give you 125 new things to do.

On the other hand, if you start with *three* strategic areas and develop *three* strategies per strategic area and *three* action steps per strategy, you get twenty-seven new things to do. This is much more realistic—and more likely to be implemented.

We do everything we can to increase the likelihood of implementation. We keep this in mind every step of the way. We are not suggesting that every strategic plan should multiply three by three by three to get to twenty-seven action steps. Think of that as a general rule of thumb to keep in mind right from the start, as these decisions are being made.

We have found that the larger and more complex the organization, the more strategic areas, strategies, and action steps they can handle. Generally speaking, we think the number of action steps ought to be limited to twenty-five to thirty. In order to reach that number, you need to begin by limiting the number of strategic areas to about three.

The number of strategic areas should be sufficiently challenging but not overwhelming. The goal of this step is to identify the most critical strategic concerns and address a reasonable number of them.

Step Four focuses on the *first* of the following three variables that *cascade* into a strategic plan:

1. Strategic Areas
2. Strategies
3. Action Steps

This and the next two steps are devoted to these three components. *Strategic areas* are defined here as the major concerns that you see as top priorities. They will become chapter headings for your strategic plan. Later, we will frame each of these concerns as *questions* facing the organization.

CONSIDER THE DATA

Attribution theory suggests that human beings tend to blame mistakes on external factors and credit internal factors to explain their successes. People often become defensive in the face of unflattering data, or dismissive of the facts that do not match the frames through which they view themselves and their organization.

When you lead a strategic planning process, you need to weigh the unflattering information right along with all the positives. Admitting a weakness is the first step toward strengthening it.

Fred facilitated a strategic planning session for an organization that surveyed customers for feedback on organizational performance and the level of client satisfaction. The response shocked and hurt the collective organizational ego. Customers complained that the organization was too slow to respond to their needs, that its product was too costly, and worst of all, that its people came across as arrogant.

The planning team's response? *"Just who do these customers think they are anyway? Who are they to make such accusations?"* It was a classic case of denial.

The team grudgingly followed Fred's recommendation to consider the unflattering input. The strategic plan included steps to counter the problems with customer service. But those in authority never fully bought into the criticism. Nor did they commit to fully implementing the steps to improve customer service. In the end, the strategic plan was a victim of the very arrogance that customers had identified at the outset.

TRANSLATE THE DATA INTO INTELLIGENCE

Once the information has been gathered, the organization needs to make sense of all that data. Leaders and managers need to convert the information into intelligence.

Information is a set of facts. Intelligence is facts placed into the context of your organization. Intelligence is influenced by time, culture, and environment.[1] Intelligence is the information that is most helpful to a strategic planning process.

The sense we make of such intelligence will shape the organization's vision and strategy. The strategic planning team needs to look hard at the organization's weaknesses as well as its strengths. You need to look hard at the threats to your organization's future well-being as well as the opportunities that may help you grow and thrive.

Strategic areas become apparent when leaders and managers make sense of the intelligence. Identifying the strategic areas is perhaps the most important decision that the strategic planning team will make. Strategic areas provide the outline for your strategic plan and the base from which your strategies and action steps will be developed.

What is the intelligence telling you about the most pressing issues facing your organization? What are the biggest questions to emerge out of the intelligence?

We recommend that you prioritize *three* strategic areas. This is not an absolute rule but a general guideline. The idea is to make the strategic plan doable. To help determine which three areas to prioritize, look at the definition of what it means to be *strategic*.

BE STRATEGIC

The Greek word *stratego* means "the general's view of the battlefield." It suggests that to be strategic is to be comprehensive, to cover the landscape, and to span the entire organization.

The word *strategic* can conjure up images of positional authority. The Greek definition gives the impression of a person with high positional authority looking down upon the people and directing the action on a battlefield. While we agree that strategic planning must take a comprehensive view and that people in positions of authority must be involved, we also think that strategic leadership can emerge from anywhere, not just from authority.

Strategic also describes something that is critical to an organization.[2] It implies a need for change. Leaders create change: a change of heart, mind, attitude, or action. In strategic planning, the focus is specific *actions* that can be taken to bring about organizational change—that is, the goals, objectives, and plans. But in the process, hearts, minds, and attitudes about the organization also change.

To be strategic, an issue has to be

- *Comprehensive*—it covers the landscape;
- *Critical*—the impact must be crucial to the organization;
- *Changeable*—it involves significant change in a positive direction; and
- *Controllable*—it is within the control of the organization.

The identification of strategic areas requires the participation of leaders who emerge from all levels of an organization. Strategic planning requires the active *participation* of a good mix of leaders, followers, and managers because the strategic areas require the serious *attention* of each of them.

THE PROCESS

In order to identify these strategic areas, go back to the environmental assessment developed in Step Two. Look at the results of your focus groups, interviews, surveys, reports, and strategic assessments to make use of your data.

We have a number of exercises for reviewing this data in order to sort for intelligence. Typically, we make sure that homework materials are sent in advance to everyone on the strategic planning team. This might include the current strategic plan, financial records, focus group reports, product and service summaries, and articles about industry trends.

At the first strategic planning session, we usually assign certain pieces of that homework to people at each table in the strategic planning room. We ask participants to review that data for ten to twelve minutes and report on its strategic importance to the rest of the strategic planning team. For example, we might ask small work groups to sift through the focus group report, assigning one or two sections from the report to each table.

The work groups study these reports for common themes, and then present what they found strategically important to the rest of the strategic planning team. This ensures that those in the group are interacting with each other and discussing the reports. It also guarantees that the team has done its homework. It informs and enlightens the next steps of the process.

After the data is reviewed for strategic significance, we have various ways of gleaning the strategic areas from all this data. We have used the MacMillan Matrix, the Balanced Scorecard, and other approaches.[3] We will present two options here:

1. The SWOT (Strengths, Weaknesses, Opportunities, and Threats) Approach
2. The Snow Card Method

1. SWOT ANALYSIS (STRENGTHS, WEAKNESSES, OPPORTUNITIES, AND THREATS)

Strengths and Weaknesses are *internal* and *present*. To explore strengths and weaknesses, look inside the organization and ask yourself, "What are we doing well?" and "What could we be doing better?"

Input from a wide representation of people, both inside and outside the organization, will ensure an honest and comprehensive list of strengths and weaknesses. Sometimes people inside the organization are too close to the work to see things clearly. Sometimes those on the ground level of the organization can see things that are not evident to those at the top.

Opportunities and Threats are *external* and *future* factors. They help us understand the wider environment in which an organization functions. They are outside forces that are impacting the organization now or that may impact it in the near future.

Opportunities are positive trends that provide fresh chances to grow the company, gain new partners, or find new resources. Threats are negative trends that create obstacles to that growth.

People sometimes confuse strengths with opportunities. They also find it hard to distinguish threats from weaknesses. Remember: both threats and opportunities are factors *outside the control* of your organization, while strengths and weaknesses are *within the control* of your organization.

The focus groups, interviews, and surveys that we conduct are often designed to identify strengths, weaknesses, opportunities, and threats (SWOT). By maximizing the participation of stakeholders inside, outside, and throughout the organization, you gain input and ownership from a wide array of people.

It is important that the senior authority make it clear that the SWOT analysis will be a free and open exchange, with no consequences for critical or negative input. We remind participants that they are being asked for this information, even negative signs such as weaknesses and threats. This is not a time for conflict avoidance. Leaders stimulate honest and thoughtful interaction on these issues.

Processing the Data. The data that has been collected and studied, as described in Step Two, is sure to be brimming with SWOT information. After closely studying this data, the strategic planning team needs to go through a process to identify the strengths, weaknesses, opportunities, and threats.

Conversation Cafés. When using the SWOT approach, we like to engage the whole team in an interactive method called *conversation cafés*. Small groups of people rotate around a set of tables where they hold conversations, as they would at a café, about the topic assigned to that table. A large chart for recording the comments of each group stays at that table. The small groups rotate around the room, adding their insights into each of the topics assigned to the tables. In short, each table becomes a *conversation café*.

Let's assume you have twenty-four people to conduct a SWOT using the conversation cafés. The next steps are as follows:

1. Divide the team into four groups of six people, each group at a separate table.
2. Place a chart at each table labeled *Strengths*, *Weaknesses*, *Opportunities*, or *Threats*.
3. Ask each work group to assign a *facilitator* to make sure everyone is participating, and a *reporter* who writes that group's ideas on the large charts.

4. Assign each group a colored marker that they will carry to each table.

5. Assign each group to a starting table. Ask them to spend about eight to ten minutes brainstorming possible ideas around the topic at that table—that is, *Strengths*, *Weaknesses*, *Opportunities*, or *Threats* —and recording their ideas on the large chart at that table.

6. Rotate the groups to each of the four tables: *Strengths*, *Weaknesses*, *Opportunities*, and *Threats*. Have them spend about eight to ten minutes adding their thoughts and ideas on the chart at each table.

7. As the work groups move from one conversation café to the next, ask the participants to first study what the previous groups have written.

8. Next, have them add their own comments and ideas. They may not erase anything a previous group has written on the charts, but they can high-light items or add comments or questions.

9. Rotate the work groups back to their original, starting tables. Ask them to review what the three other groups have added to the chart they started. Have them spend about eight to ten minutes look-ing for two to three major themes on that chart. Find some white space on the large chart to write in these themes in large and colorful lettering.

10. Ask each work group to present their findings to the full team. This helps prioritize the SWOT and leads to a more complete assessment before identi-fying the strategic areas.

We assign a different colored marker to each work group so we can differentiate each group's comments. If a question is raised about something written on a chart, the facilitator can find someone from that work group to explain the comment.

Remind people that the strengths and weaknesses are *internal*. They are within your organization's control. The opportunities and threats are *external*. They are outside your control.

It should be noted that the adage, *our best strengths can be our very weaknesses*, is often proven true by this process. An organization rooted in long-standing tradition often points to its history as a strength. But being rooted in tradition may also be a weakness if that organization is unwilling to change and adapt to new realities.

The Gallery Walk. When using the conversation cafés, we follow them up with another interactive method that we call the *gallery walk*. This is particularly helpful to the visual learners on the team. The artwork for this gallery is the four colorful charts that emerge out of the conversation cafés—those depicting the SWOT analysis.

The four charts are posted on a wall that becomes our *gallery*. The strategic planning team studies the colorful charts, looking for overall themes, conversing with each other, and comparing and contrasting the *strengths*, *weaknesses*, *opportunities*, and *threats* suggested on the charts. For some people, the strategic areas just seem to pop out of this data. It helps them to make the connections and see the bigger picture.

As the strategic planning team walks around the gallery, ask them to look for strategic areas that seem to emerge from the data. For the strategic thinkers in the room, the strategic areas often become obvious as they walk about the room and study the charts.

This is also a good time to remind the team what it means to be *strategic*. Remember that to be strategic, an issue needs to be *comprehensive* and *critical*. It needs to involve *change* and be within your *control*.

Use the SWOT to Find the Strategic Areas. As you search for strategic areas, it is helpful to compare and contrast your internal strengths and weaknesses with the external opportunities and threats—that is, how do your strengths match up with potential opportunities?

To use a basketball analogy: if your strength is a tall and athletic center who can score, and your opponent has a weak center, your strategy is to get the ball to your center. Your opponent's weakness is your opportunity. Your opponent's strength is your threat.

If an external threat matches an organizational weakness, the discussion might center on how the organization can protect itself from that threat. Can the organization transform that weakness into a strength? If so, is it worth the time, effort, and expense to address that weakness in order to protect the organization from a threat, or to capitalize on an opportunity?

Another pertinent question is what are your competitors' strengths and weaknesses? The weaknesses of your competition create opportunities for your growth. The strengths of your competition create obstacles to your growth. They can be viewed as threats.

Strategic Question. After the gallery walk, we ask participants to form small work groups to discuss the possible strategic areas. We ask them to consider these questions:

- Based on the information on the SWOT analysis, what do you think are the two or three major issues, questions, or challenges facing your organization?
- What would be the two or three major categories of your strategic plan?

We ask each work group to articulate these major challenges as strategic questions starting with these three words:

"*How can we...?*"[4] At each table, the group decides upon two or three strategic questions and reports those to the full group.

As the ideas are reported, a volunteer writes down (in a place where everyone can see it) a key word or phrase depicting each idea. In some cases, similar ideas are suggested and the facilitator can test whether the strategic planning team wants to group some of these ideas together or not. This should be a team decision. Too much grouping can lose the unique character of a strategic idea.

In most cases, the work groups suggest very similar ideas and consensus comes easily. However, we have experienced high levels of conflict at this stage as well. This requires good facilitation. It is important that all views are expressed as the entire strategic planning team works together to reach consensus on determining the three strategic areas.

2. THE SNOW CARD METHOD

Another approach to identifying the strategic areas is the *snow card*.[5] Some groups prefer this method as it immediately gets into the heart of the major issues, challenges, and concerns facing the organization. In most cases, the snow card method moves more quickly than the SWOT approach with its conversation cafés and gallery walk.

As with the SWOT approach, the goal of the snow card process is to translate the data into intelligence and generalize the intelligence into three strategic areas. By the end of this step, the team will identify three strategic areas and articulate them as strategic questions.

As with SWOT, this process works best if the data has been collected from a variety of sources and analyzed by all participants. Everyone needs to do his or her homework. Before starting the snow card process, it is best for the strategic planning team to go through a process such as the one described above to review and study the homework and sort for intelligence.

The snow card technique begins with the distribution of note cards, or pads of sticky notes, to each participant. People are asked to write one thought on each card answering the question, *what are the main issues, challenges, or questions facing this organization?*

At this point, it is important to remind everyone that participants must feel free to state what is on their minds. It is helpful for the senior authority to encourage people to speak freely and to be open to constructive feedback so people are less afraid of repercussions.

Ideas written on the snow cards can encompass anything that might be of strategic importance—process issues, program concerns, product questions, leadership challenges. Anything that could affect the future of the organization should be shared.

We ask participants to think about what keeps them up at night and to write those things down, one thought per sticky note. For about fifteen to twenty minutes, the participants write down their thoughts and randomly post the sticky notes on an open wall. The result is what gives this process its name, as the dozens of notes appear to be like *snowflakes* falling across the sky.

One advantage to using the snow card process is the greater inclusion of quieter participants who might feel intimidated by the rapid-fire discussion that can occur in the conversation cafés. Those who are more extroverted sometimes think aloud about their thoughts and can dominate discussions. The snow card technique opens up more room for participation from all members of the strategic planning team.

Categorize the Issues. The next step is to make sense of the different issues identified on the snow cards. At this point, we ask for five or six volunteers to review the snow cards, organize them into themes, and identify names for the various categories. They are looking for common themes that will become the strategic areas of your plan.

It is important to recruit a diverse group of volunteers for this process: leaders and managers, people from various departments, those with experience, and those who are new. It is also important to facilitate this discussion so that everyone's viewpoint can be heard.

Categories are not specified in advance but are developed in an inductive manner, which means they emerge out of the data. The volunteers scan the snow cards, looking for similarities. As they begin to see the major themes, we ask the volunteers to literally move the snow cards around and group them together under the emerging categories.

The following are categories that might be included:

- Programs, Products, or Services
- Organizational Processes
- Recruitment of New Talent
- Employee Relations
- Training Needs
- Reward Structure
- Facilities
- Information Technology
- Leadership
- Communication
- Marketing
- Resources

This categorization process normally takes fifteen to twenty minutes. When finished, too many categories have usually emerged. As with the SWOT analysis, identifying too many strategic areas will overwhelm the rest of the process. So the next step in the snow card method is to consolidate the material into three categories. Some possible groupings are:

- Can marketing be combined with communication?
- Can information technology be paired with facilities?
- Can recruitment, retention, training, and reward structure for employees be consolidated into one category on human resources?

Our general rule is to strive for consolidation into three strategic areas. The more strategic areas you add, the more likely you are to end up with too many strategies and action items to implement all of them.

Strategic Questions. Once the team has reached consensus on three strategic areas, the final part of this step is to articulate the three areas as strategic questions starting with the three words, *"How can we…?"* We assign each category to a small work group and ask them to study the topic in greater detail. Look at the snow cards that were grouped into that category and discuss these questions:

- What do the snow cards mean?
- What are they telling us?
- What do we need to do about them?

We instruct the work groups to craft a positively worded sentence to capture the essence of that issue. For example, the question might read, *"How can we* diversify our sources of funding *so that we* are more financially stable?" It is important in this step to remain focused on the big picture, not to be sidetracked by the tiny details.

PROCESS CHECK

Once consensus has been reached on three strategic areas, two or three volunteers take the notes from the discussion and wordsmith the strategic questions. If this is the conclusion of the first strategic planning session, this task can be done at a separate meeting or worked online. Otherwise, it can be done while the rest of the group takes a break.

Wordsmithing is not a large group activity. Don't waste precious time working on small changes in wording. The best way to evaluate a *"How can we?"* question is to ask whether it stimulates the discussion we need in the next step of the process: *answer the questions.*

CONCLUSION

The strategic planning team at LMX had a difficult time sorting through its many varied concerns and multiple interests to prioritize only three strategic areas. Once they had reached that goal, they knew they had turned a corner. The process had forced them to focus their energies on what was most urgent, important, and realistic.

Identifying the strategic areas is a turning point in our strategic planning process. In this step, the strategic planning team decides which three issues will become the priorities. Those three issues become the focal point for future activities, the areas to invest new resources, and the cornerstones of the strategic plan.

What LMX learned from this exercise is that strategic areas need to be strategic. It is important that they significantly impact the entire organization—not just one division, department, or program. What's more, they need to rise above the level of operations and into the realm of strategic change. LMX had ended the first strategic planning meeting by framing the questions that will be answered in the next step: *developing strategies to answer the strategic questions.*

ANSWER THE QUESTIONS

Develop Strategies

"If you don't get up every morning with a burning desire to do things, you don't have enough goals."
—Lou Holtz

Family Resources Inc. (FRI) found itself facing the same question as many large social service agencies: *How can we find new and diverse sources of revenue, given the increasingly competitive nature of our business?*

The FRI leaders knew this issue was a matter of utmost importance. But an agency handling hundreds of the most difficult children's cases in the state of Iowa had precious little time to address it. They found themselves relying increasingly on government sources of funding, even though everyone in the organization was worried about how long that could last.

Like FRI, many not-for-profit organizations rely too heavily on one source of funding. Unlike FRI, some borrow from reserves to get through one year, and the next, and the next. Eventually, the reserves run dry. Something has to be done.

For-profit businesses can face this same dilemma if they rely too heavily on one customer. Eventually, that one customer might realize just how dependent the company is. And they can negotiate business terms from a position of strength. This makes the business weak and vulnerable.

At FRI, the leaders faced the reality of the situation. The strategic planning process creates the moment of truth and is the time to confront the reality of the strategic areas.

URGENT AND IMPORTANT

Leaders develop a sense of urgency about what is most important.[1] With all the urgent issues people face each day, it is easy to be caught up in the crisis of the moment. That is why it is important to have both *effective leadership* and *efficient management*. Managers handle the day-to-day crises that are urgent. Leaders look strategically at the organization and make sure attention also is directed toward issues that are *important but not necessarily urgent*—such as the strategic areas you identified in the previous step.[2]

Step Five responds to your strategic issues. Strategic planning is the time to get away from the crisis mode and think strategically as a team about how to address the important questions that have been nagging you for some time.

Our process is designed to help you find synergy as a team. You want to explore new ways of thinking about your strategic areas and surface new ideas to solve them. With the right people at the table, you will generate buy-in and support for these new strategies. This sense of ownership will be needed when we get to implementation.

Remember also that leaders inspire people to think *outside the box but inside the circle* (see Figure 2 on page 15). Create enough space for creative thinking that is outside the way your organization usually does things (the box), but inside the parameters set by your policies, mandates, rules, core mission, and values (the circle).

DEVELOP THE STRATEGIC CASCADE

Once the strategic areas have been identified as strategic questions, the next step is to try to answer those questions with strategies. This begins the *problem-solving* part of our process.

We call the strategic areas, strategies, and action steps a *strategic cascade* because the actions to be taken flow *like a waterfall*, going from strategic area to strategy to action step, each time with more and more specificity:

- Each Strategic Area has a set of *Strategies*.
- Each Strategy has its own set of *Action Steps*.

This creates a cascading effect, if you will. Different organizations prefer different terms. But the process should always result in going from general areas to specific steps.

Strategic Goals. Once the strategic planning team has articulated the strategic areas as strategic questions, we suggest that you begin to use the term *strategic goals*, which are the strategic questions without the three words, *"How can we…?"*

Simply put, *"How can we* establish a new brand for our organization?" becomes "Establish a new brand for our organization." We will refer to this as your strategic goal.

As facilitators, we can adapt and use whatever terminology an organization prefers. The important thing is that we get more and more specific—cascading into specific steps to take and specific measures of success.

ROLE OF THE FACILITATOR

Whether we use the conversation cafés or the snow card technique in this step, we ask each small work group to identify (1) a facilitator, (2) a timekeeper, and (3) a notetaker for this process. It is important that people other than the group facilitator watch the time and take notes—so the facilitator can concentrate solely on facilitation.

Work group facilitators:

- Call people by name throughout the meeting;
- Keep the focus on topic;
- Listen carefully to what is being said;
- Summarize the comments briefly to test for understanding;
- Call on the quieter ones;
- Keep things moving in a timely fashion; and
- Conclude by thanking everyone for participating.

To make sure that everyone is paying close attention to each other, it is important that facilitators occasionally summarize what has already been said. If conflict occurs, the facilitator might want to ask each of the conflicted parties to summarize what the other is saying.

At times, the facilitator needs to remind the team that everyone should have an opportunity to speak. Dominant parties should be asked to monitor their input. When necessary, the facilitator might even need to interrupt dominant parties—with tact and grace.

THE SNOW CARD METHOD

Once the work groups have crafted the strategic questions from the previous step, and the full strategic planning team has adopted those as three strategic goals, the same work groups are reconvened to develop three possible strategies for each strategic goal.

We reconvene the same people that developed the strategic questions. This time they look for three specific topics that will become strategies. We ask the groups to look at the dozens of snow cards for each strategic goal and have a conversation around these questions:

- What are the snow cards telling us?
- What do they mean?
- What do we need to do about them?

The work groups have this discussion while studying the sticky notes for each strategic goal. They need to establish three *primary themes* from the discussion.

For example, a work group identified a strategic area of "Human Resources" and a strategic goal of "Improve our HR Systems." They might break the notes into subcategories of hiring, retention, and annual appraisals. The group develops three HR strategies, such as "Revamp our hiring process," "Build stronger relationships in our work teams," and "Improve our annual appraisal forms." You can see that these strategies fit under the general topic of HR—but they are not yet specific or measurable.

As with the strategic goals, it is important not to develop too many subcategories. We remind the work groups to limit their results to no more than three strategies per strategic goal.

When the work groups are finished, they reconvene to the full team where each group reports its three proposed strategies. Upon hearing the report from the work groups, it is the decision of the full strategic planning team to affirm or change these three ideas as *strategies* moving forward.

CONVERSATION CAFÉS

Another way to develop the strategies for each strategic goal is to hold a round of conversation cafés. In this approach, small work groups rotate among tables that are each designated as a different strategic goal, instead of being assigned to work on one strategic goal.

One advantage of the conversation cafés approach is that it provides an opportunity for each participant to continue to have input into each of the strategic goals. The disadvantage is that conversation cafés may take more time.

To organize the conversation cafés, the facilitator writes the names of the three strategic goals at the top of three large charts, each followed by the strategic question that goes with it. For example, one chart might say, "Growth: How can we expand into new geographic territories in order to grow the company?" One chart is placed at the center of each table in the room.

If the strategic planning team is larger than about twenty-four people, the facilitator needs to consider ways of adjusting to the size of the team. As the team gets larger, the facilitator has to figure out ways of keeping the advantages of smaller group inter-action. One possibility is to set up two or three tables for each strategic goal—and then coordinate the work among those tables as an extra step.

Let's assume the strategic planning team has twenty-four members and has identified three strategic goals. In that case, we would place the participants into three groups of eight people per table. These three work groups would rotate around to all three tables.

As in the previous set of conversation cafés, each work group selects a facilitator, a timekeeper, and a scribe. Each group is also assigned a different color marker. That way, as the groups rotate among the tables, participants can track down the author of an idea that might have been expressed by a previous group. Participants add their thoughts and ideas to each idea on the chart at that table. The result is a colorful collection of ideas that expresses the synergy and consensus of the full strategic planning team.

At each table, the work group has a conversation, as one would at a café, about ways to answer the question at that table. The tables become like cafés for a conversation about each strategic goal. These conversations usually take about twelve to fifteen minutes until the groups rotate to the next table and consider the next strategic question.

The work groups are asked to brainstorm ways to answer each strategic question. Ideas are *not* assessed for their strengths and weaknesses. This will come later. It is best to keep the flow of conversation going. This helps build a high level of synergy where one idea builds upon the other. It takes good facilitation to keep the flow of conversation going.

At this point, we do not insist that each strategy has to be measurable. Insisting on too many criteria at this point only slows down the process. It stifles creative thinking. Measurability will come later.

As participants express one idea after another, the scribe writes down the ideas on the group's chart. Only questions of clarification are asked at this point. Questions about whether the idea is realistic, optimal, measurable, or strategic will be addressed later.

As the work groups rotate to each new table, they are asked to first study the results of the previous groups whose input already is on that chart. This extends the conversation about that strategic goal to the other work groups as well.

After reading the material from previous work groups, participants use their own colors to add their own ideas about answering the strategic question. The result is a very colorful display of ideas and input about each strategic goal.

Once the rotation among the tables is completed, each work group returns to its original table. Members study the colorful results. They see how their original ideas stimulated the other work groups to reach an array of ideas to answer that strategic question.

As with the snow card technique, the final step in the conversation cafés is that each work group is asked to search that original chart for two to four *primary themes* that have emerged out of the brainstorming sessions.

LARGE GROUP REPORT

Once the strategies have been developed by the work groups, they need to be reported back to the whole team for consensus.[3] Regardless of the method used to surface the strategies, each work group now reports on the two to four themes that emerged out of the discussions.

Facilitation is key to making this step work. Reaching consensus will build a sense of ownership in the plan. It is important that enough time and discussion is allowed for the full team to come to consensus so that everyone buys into these ideas as primary themes. These themes will become the strategies for the strategic goals.

When the work groups have finished their work on the strategic goals, everyone reconvenes as the strategic planning team. Each work group presents their findings to the whole team. The facilitator helps the team reach consensus on each strategy, one at a time. This gives everyone a chance to hear, comment on, and buy into the results.

CHECKING BACK WITH OTHER STAKEHOLDERS

Another step that we recommend was initially suggested to us by the strategic planning team at Black Hawk College. Once the strategic planning team had identified the three strategic goals, Dan was asked to re-interview the participants in the focus groups.

The idea was to double check with these stakeholders about: (a) whether they thought the planning team had identified the right strategic goals; and (b) what suggestions they had to respond to the strategic questions that had been developed by the planning team.

This additional step adds credibility to the entire process. It gives the strategic planning team more input into possible strategies going forward. And it adds a greater sense of owner-ship of the eventual plan to even more stakeholders.

PROCESS CHECK

At this point, the strategic planning team has identified:

- Three strategic goals; and
- Three strategies per strategic goal.

The next step will be to develop

- Three action steps per strategy.

Strategic plans move from general to specific. The next step in cascading the plan will be to *get specific*—when we identify several action steps per strategy. Without specificity, a vision is just an illusion. Without a specific action plan, the strategic plan will become the dreaded coffee table decoration. It is unlikely to be implemented.

Below is a representative display of what the strategic cas-cade might look like.

Figure 5: Strategic Cascade

CONCLUSION

Family Resources Inc. (FRI) went through this process and identified *Diversify Sources of Funding* as a strategic goal. Their most promising strategy was to do more fundraising by soliciting major gifts. After all, the cheapest, fastest, and most effective way to fundraise is to ask. FRI still faces difficult times ahead with public funding uncertainties but is facing the reality of their current environment by investing resources into raising more private donations.

The content of the best strategies depends on the imagination and expertise of the strategic planning team. Our process contributes the opportunity for the leaders, managers, and members of an organization to interact. At FRI, we found that the best answers to the most perplexing strategic questions evolved out of the interaction of the planning team. In fact, the conversations among team members raised the sense of urgency to get the job done.

This is one way that we differ from many strategic planning consultants. We are not *content* experts. We are *process* experts. We cannot and will not tell the strategic planning team what to do about their most difficult issues. Instead, we structure the planning process so that the very best answers come from the participants themselves. The people at FRI know firsthand what is working and where the organizational problems are. Participation from people who are in the trenches is a core value for us.

We feel that the snow card technique, conversation cafés, and gallery walks described in this step offer an engaging way to involve large numbers of people in deciding upon the best strategies. In the process of developing the strategic plan, the vision is cocreated by the whole strategic planning team—not by one or two people.

GET SPECIFIC

Write Out the Action Steps

"Action will delineate and define you."
—Thomas Jefferson

The LMX strategic planning team had struggled mightily to limit themselves to only three strategic goals. Given the huge challenges facing LMX, it seemed almost impossible to limit the strategic goals to three. But they had accomplished the impossible.

Not only that, they had also limited their strategies to only three per strategic goal. The strategic planning team had a sense of optimism that had seemed very unlikely a few hours ago. They had confronted the reality of their most pressing issues while making the difficult decision to prioritize and therefore limit their strategic goals and strategies.

Their three strategic goals and three strategies per strategic goal were locked and ready to go. As they headed into the action stage, they realized the wisdom of prioritization. If they had decided upon five strategic goals and added five strategies per strategic goal, they would now have twenty-five new strategies! Imagine adding three action steps to each of twenty-five strategies. That would have resulted in seventy-five action items.

As it was, LMX had nine strategies. Adding three action items to each strategy would result in twenty-seven action steps. Much more realistic.

Some organizations stop when they have identified their strategies. But strategies do not have to be specific, so stopping at this point runs the risk of adopting a strategic plan that is not measurable.

In Step Four, strategic planning teams often design strategic goals such as empowering staff, delegating more responsibility, or changing the way we conduct meetings. These are worthy ideas but are too ambiguous to measure. In Step Five, the strategies do not have to be specific either. They do not have to be measurable. They give us a general idea of how to answer our strategic questions.

In Step Six, we *get specific*. Now we get to measurable actions. It is time to write the *action steps*.

It never ceases to amaze us how many organizations develop strategic plans but fail to implement them. Even after investing valuable time and energy in developing the strategic plan, many organizations continue to operate as if the strategic planning process never happened. Research shows that 70 to 90 percent of strategic plans are not implemented.[1]

There are many reasons for this. In some cases, the environment changes so quickly that the strategic plan becomes outdated. In other cases, the resources needed to implement the plan are not available. But more often than not, strategic plans do not get implemented because they lack an action plan. They lack specificity and measurability.

We cannot stress this enough:

Any plan worth planning is worth implementing.

THE ACTION PLAN

Action steps include three criteria:

- What (specifically) is going to be done?
- Who is going to be responsible for getting it done?
- By when?

One way to ensure measurability is to design the action steps as what we call a "*Go/No-Go*." These are actions that are so specific that everyone knows whether they have been done or not: Remodel a building. Hire a person. Hold an event. Launch a new product. Put up a billboard. Later, you can ask yourself whether the action was a "Go" or a "No-Go."

Some action steps can also be quantified, such as "Launch three new products in the next twelve months," or "Hire four new people in the next six months." Write the action steps so that you can tell later whether each step was successful or not. Knowing whether the step taken was a "Go" or a "No-Go" will help ensure implementation. That builds accountability into the action steps.

Accountability also includes assigning two people to be responsible for each item. In our system, those two will be responsible for reporting on that item when the planning team gathers together to review, evaluate, and update the strategic plan. We schedule such reviews—which we call accountability sessions—every three months.

We also ask that each item be assigned a timeline of three, six, nine, or twelve months. Anything that is going to take longer than twelve months is generally excluded from the action-step timeline. Instead, we like to break down those longer-range activities and ask what interim steps will be completed to move us in the direction of each longer-term step.

The two people assigned to an action item might be a board member and a staff member. They might be a leader and a manager. They might be the one person who is responsible for *doing* the action or *taking* the step and one person responsible for *overseeing* that action item. Both need to share an interest in the action item.

Remember, it is important that your strategic planning team has a good mix of leaders and followers, managers and workers, including the following:

- Those who see the big picture and how the action steps fit with the strategic goals
- Those who understand the tiny details of day-to-day implementation

THE PROCESS

Set up a small work group for each strategic goal. Create three large charts that look like Figure 6. At the top of each chart, write the name of the strategic goal. Next, add the three strategies under that strategic goal. Then, ask the work groups to fill in the blanks next to each strategy, including (1) a specific action step, (2) a timeline at three, six, nine, or twelve months, and (3) the names of two people who will be the contact persons for that step. *Note*: We remind the work groups that three action items per strategy is a general guideline, not an absolute rule. We are shooting for *about nine* action steps per strategic goal.

In this step, the work groups will *not* rotate between all three tables, so it is important to get the right people at each table. We ask people to select for themselves the table at which they want to work, within three constraints:

Action Plan

1) Write in Name of Strategic Goal #1
1.1 Write in Name of Strategy 1.1
    1.1.1_____
    1.1.2_____
    1.1.3_____
1.2 Write in Name of Strategy 1.2
    1.2.1_____
    1.2.2_____
    1.2.3_____
1.3 Write in Name of Strategy 1.3
    1.3.1_____
    1.3.2_____
    1.3.3_____

2) Write in Name of Strategic Goal #2
2.1 Write in Name of Strategy 2.1
    2.1.1_____
    2.1.2_____
    2.1.3_____
2.2 Write in Name of Strategy 2.2
    2.2.1_____
    2.2.2_____
    2.2.3_____
2.3 Write in Name of Strategy 2.3
    2.3.1_____
    2.3.2_____
    2.3.3_____

3) Write in Name of Strategic Goal #3
3.1 Write in Name of Strategy 3.1
    3.1.1_____
    3.1.2_____
    3.1.3_____
3.2 Write in Name of Strategy 3.2
    3.2.1_____
    3.2.2_____
    3.2.3_____
3.3 Write in Name of Strategy 3.3
    3.3.1_____
    3.3.2_____
    3.3.3_____

Figure 6: Forms to be completed for Action Plan

1. Ask key people who have a major role in a certain strategic goal to participate at that table. For example, if the strategic goal is marketing, and the organization has a director of marketing, we want that person to work on marketing.
2. Consider diversity at each table. For example, if the strategic planning team has board members and paid staff, get a good representation from both groups at each table.
3. Put a similar number of people at each table. For example, if raising income from diverse sources of revenue is a strategic goal, make sure that enough people are at that table to create that action plan.

Because the work groups will not rotate among all three tables, it is important to ask some key people, such as the CEO and chair of the board, to walk around the room, participating in conversations occurring at all three tables. This helps ensure that the action items are

- New (that activity is not already being done);
- Realistic (there are enough resources to carry it out);
- Timely (it does not conflict with other plans); and
- Properly delegated (the right people have been assigned to it).

Facilitators also rotate among the three tables, ensuring that

- Planners for each strategic goal are clear about the assignment;
- Each work group is well-facilitated and participation is lively; and
- Planners at one table are not duplicating what another group is doing.

Communication among the three tables is important through this process. For example, if someone at one table wants to write down the name of a person at another table as the contact person for a certain action item, ask that person first. If two work groups are planning actions for a similar effort, coordinate between the two tables to avoid duplication of effort.

Once the three work groups have finished their action items, ask each group to present its action plan to the full planning team for further discussion, clarification, and approval.

ACCOUNTABILITY SESSIONS

Once the strategic plan has been adopted and the implementation begins, the action plan becomes the critical point of evaluation. We schedule *accountability sessions*, which are quarterly meetings of the strategic planning team, to monitor progress on the strategic plan (see Step Eight for a full description of these sessions).

At these meetings, look at each action item that was supposed to be completed according to the schedule stated in Step Six. Ask the contact person on that item for a progress report. This is why the action items need to be specific, with the name of a contact person and a timeline for each item. That is what makes the plan measurable.

Specificity leads to measurability, which leads to accountability.

LEADERSHIP AGENDA

Another step to implementation is to keep the strategic plan on the agenda for meetings of leaders and managers. The strategic goals should become the outline for the agenda for meetings of the top decision makers in the organization.

If the strategic goals are indeed *strategic*, then they should be the most urgent and important issues facing the organization. If they are not perceived as urgent *and* important, the leaders need to change that perception. Leaders urge people to focus on what is important.

If the executives are spending a significant amount of time on a matter that is unrelated to the strategic goals, then one of two things has happened:

1. They have veered away from the most urgent and important issues; or
2. They have identified another strategic goal that needs to be addressed.

If the leaders and managers are focusing on something that is not strategic, then someone in leadership needs to challenge the team to refocus on the most strategic and important issues. If a new strategic goal has been identified, the strategic plan needs to be updated.

DASHBOARD MEASURES

Another way to ensure implementation is to use dashboards to monitor progress on the strategies and action steps. We like the colored versions that use green lights to indicate steady progress, yellow lights to indicate caution or concern, and red lights to indicate roadblocks.[2]

Progress on a strategic plan is more likely if the action steps are used in performance standards. Those in authority should use the strategic plan in setting their own goals as well as the goals for people they supervise. This is a best practice for strategic planning. Aligning the organizational strategies and action steps with the annual goals of the workforce increases the likelihood of implementation and accountability.

Some organizations designate certain committees or work project teams for each strategic goal. They make sure that people from all levels of the organization—staff, managers, board members, owners, and all stakeholders—are involved in some of the implementation. When the update on those action items is provided to the strategic planning team, anyone can present the update—not just the senior authorities.

OUR CONSTANTLY CHANGING WORLD

Changes in the external environment are one reason that people decide to do strategic planning. However, these changes can also become a major obstacle to implementation. If changes occur shortly after the strategic planning process, then adjustments become necessary.

Dan was working for an organization that lost a major source of funding within six months of strategic planning. This led to more intense accountability sessions. Eventually, the organization invited Dan back to do a one-year update of the strategic plan—complete with another round of focus groups and one-on-one interviews. This helped the organization continue to adapt to its external changes.

Strategic planning prepares the organization to protect against such threats when and if they appear. We have seen leaders and managers who are much more prepared to adjust to changes in the external environment after they go through this interactive strategic planning process. Strategic planning helps prepare the organization for strategic thinking.

Similarly, organizations will be much more prepared to pursue new opportunities that present themselves after the strategic planning process. We have seen this occur many times: An organization goes through strategic planning. A new opportunity emerges shortly afterward. Because of the planning process, the leaders and managers are much more prepared to make strategic decisions—and are more trusting of each other while making those decisions.

GENERATING TASK CONFLICT

By facing the reality of situations that are often ignored or downplayed, strategic planning can generate conflict within the organization. We have had several experiences where an organization called us back within several months of strategic planning to do conflict negotiation or mediation.

When people are overly agreeable, or conflict-avoidant, the best ideas fail to surface. This can result in groupthink—where everyone thinks alike. It is healthy to be suspicious of a unanimous decision and to ask whether the decision was premature.

Generating *task conflict* is one of the most important activities of a leader. The key is to stimulate, monitor, and deal constructively with task conflict without allowing it to become *relationship conflict*.[3] Task conflict happens when people have different opinions about how to complete the task or solve the problem. Relationship conflict occurs when people attack one another instead of attacking the problem.

Research shows that small to moderate amounts of *task* conflict are healthy for teams and organizations.[4] If your strategic planning team lacks task conflict, you are probably missing something. Without task conflict, you are likely to devolve into groupthink. However, research also shows that *relationship* conflict in any amount is not healthy.[5] Relationship conflict can grow when task conflict is not resolved but instead escalates into people problems.

When people see task conflict as a positive thing, it is less likely that differences of opinion will lead to relationship conflict.

Leaders have to create an environment where differences of opinion on tasks are encouraged and appreciated. The key is to be assertive about your own needs and interests while also being mindful of the needs and interests of others.[6]

RESOLVING PERSONAL CONFLICTS

Change is laden with conflict, and strategic planning can expose both task and relationship conflict. Some of these conflicts become clear to us from Step One. For example, if a key authority person in the organization is not among the representatives who meet with us to do the initial planning, it can be a red flag.

Dan conducted planning for an organization that purposely excluded the CEO. In fact, board members had been asking for a strategic planning process for years but the CEO refused. Dan probed the board about their roles and responsibilities. Eventually, the board took the drastic step of firing the CEO. Several months later, they were able to go through a strategic planning process with a new CEO.

Dan had another experience where a vice president was dragging her feet about strategic planning. She was very quiet throughout the process. She was merely going through the motions. She was thinking inside her own silo and protecting her own turf. She appeared to be resistant to change. Nevertheless, the strategic planning team went ahead and wrote some major changes into the strategic plan that affected her department.

When it came to implementation, the conflict burst wide open. She had no intention of implementing the strategic change. In retrospect, we found that she had figured she would just allow the strategic planning process to move forward, and that no one would notice if the change was not implemented. This is *passive aggressive* behavior.

Eventually, Dan was called back to conduct conflict mediation between the CEO and the VP. The task conflict had escalated into relationship conflict. When this happens, the results can be destructive to the entire team or organization. With careful mediation, we were able to reestablish lines of communication. Once the CEO fully listened to the VP's concerns and demonstrated understanding, the VP eventually bought into the strategic plan.

Resistance to change is one reason that some action steps should be taken within the first three months. It is important to expose that resistance sooner rather than later. Often the conflict surfaces at the first accountability session when it becomes apparent that no action has been taken.

We find that the participatory process we conduct, and the enthusiasm it generates, usually changes the negative attitude of a change resister. The strategic planning process described in this book allows for everyone to make their cases and for all viewpoints to be heard.

People are more likely to resist change when

1. They are not involved in the change process;
2. They do not trust those in authority; or
3. The change signifies loss of an important interest.

To overcome these obstacles to change, leaders do the following:

1. *Involve people* in the change process—especially those who will be involved in the implementation. If you want people to be the change you wish to see, as Gandhi suggests, then involve them in that change. You will gain more ownership as they buy into the change.

2. *Act in a trustworthy manner.* If the process is honest, open, and transparent, you will gain more credibility and build more trust.
3. *Look for collaborative solutions* that meet mutual interests. When leading a strategic planning process, keep searching for win-win solutions.[7] Make solving someone else's problem your problem. Help them win as you win.

PROCESS CHECK

The development of the action plan, with its specific steps that can be implemented and measured, concludes the *strategic cascade* of strategic goals, strategies, and action steps. At this point, the strategic planning team might think their job is done. They are very close.

But before adjourning, we engage the strategic planning team in one last step: *discovering the vision.* At this point, the team has actually cocreated a new vision for the organization. The next step will be to capture the essence of that vision and bring some closure to the planning process by articulating a vision statement.

CONCLUSION

LMX had entered the strategic planning process worried that so many pressing challenges would make strategic planning impossible: How could they agree to limit their strategic goals and strategies? Our interactive planning process created the environment for these difficult decisions to be made—and to involve many stakeholders in the process.

The importance of limiting the strategic goals and strategies becomes clear when you get around to writing the action steps. Many strategic plans fail because they are already too long before they even get to this step. The LMX team was able to keep their plan doable. This step was actually easy because the difficult decisions had been made earlier.

However, too many organizations go through the entire strategic planning process and then fail to get specific about what action steps they will take. The lack of specificity in the action plan is the greatest obstacle to implementing the strategic plan.

Our process is designed to maximize the likelihood of implementation. Identifying specific steps in the action plan creates the framework for accountability for implementation. Once the action steps are listed in the plan, the strategic planning team should meet quarterly to review, update, and revise the plan. This ensures that the plan is a living, breathing document, not something to be lost on someone's hard drive. Accountability sessions should be lively events with open, honest exchange about what has or has not been done, what is being done, and what needs to be done.

DISCOVER THE VISION

Craft the Vision Statement

"Where there is no vision the people perish."
—Proverbs 29:18

As a teenager, Chad Pregracke had a vision. He wanted to clean the Mississippi River. That is a big vision, of course. It is a big river. His first inclination was to start cleaning the river himself: one person, one boat, one day at a time, one piece of junk at a time.

Eventually, he realized that was not enough. The change he wanted to see was too big for one person. So in 1998, at the age of twenty-three, he formed Living Lands and Waters, a not-for-profit organization that has sponsored more than seven hundred clean-ups, involving tens of thousands of volunteers, on twenty-three different rivers over the past twenty years.[1] In 2013, Chad Pregracke was selected as the CNN Hero of the Year. Not bad for a kid who started out working as a shell diver.

How did Chad accomplish so much? How was he able to make the transition from one person picking up one muck-filled tire at a time to a multimillion dollar not-for-profit organization with more than seventy thousand volunteers?

What is amazing about Chad's story is how he was able to make the leap from personal activism to leadership. Like almost anyone who accomplishes great things, Chad started with a vision.

But he didn't stop there. He also led his people through the strategic planning process described in this book.

Involving others in developing the plan toward his vision is one way that Chad made the leap from a one-man show to one man leading thousands of others. He learned how to inspire others to share, expand, and join in his vision, and those others helped him cocreate a new vision.

VISIONARY LEADERS

We ask students in our strategic planning classes to select and write about a leader they consider visionary. This exercise tends to produce an eclectic and impressive group of subjects, and the explanations for these visionary choices are equally wide-ranging.

Several traits are associated with visionary leaders who are successful.

- *Passionate*—they care deeply about mission and core values
- *Eloquent*—they describe the future so distinctly that people can see it
- *Honest*—they inspire trust
- *Inspiring*—they intrinsically motivate others to join them
- *Persistent*—they don't give up
- *Forward-Looking*—they pay attention to trends in their businesses

FORWARD-LOOKING LEADERS

Research shows that being *forward-looking* is one of the four most admired leadership traits.[2] The others are being honest, competent, and inspiring. These traits are acquired, not inborn. People are *not* born leaders. That is a myth. People may be born with potential for developing certain leadership traits, but that does not mean they are born leaders. Leadership traits are developed over time. People are not born patient, wise, and courageous. Virtuous traits are developed by practicing virtuous behaviors—and by reflecting on these practices.

Leaders want to thrive, not simply survive. Leaders see the big picture and focus on the future. They ask the following: Where are we now? Where are we headed? What is changing in our environment? How has our business changed? What is changing now? What is the next big challenge on our horizon?

Forward-looking leaders

- Realize that the world is moving fast;
- Prioritize their time to think about the future;
- Step up and ask the tough questions;
- Stimulate task conflict by encouraging divergent ideas; and
- Challenge resistance to change.

Most people are wired to accept the status quo. *People will resist change—particularly the change they don't choose.* By involving people in the change process, leaders can neutralize some of that resistance.

Remember that *entropy* suggests that every organization is in the process of dying. Entropic forces are changing your reality. They are forcing you to change. Unless you breathe new life into your organization, it will die. Unless you keep up with the changing times, your organization will cease to exist—or cease to have a reason to exist.

Leaders sharpen the strategic saws by spending time each day asking, "What are the biggest changes occurring in the world today, those that will impact this organization in three, five, or ten years?" Read the news each day and ask yourself, "What stories today will impact my profession, my business, or my organization in the next three, five, and ten years?" Leaders act themselves into a new way of thinking and being.

THE IMPORTANCE OF VISION

Alice speaks to the Cheshire Cat:

"Would you tell me, please, which way I ought to go from here?"

"That depends a good deal on where you want to get to," said the Cat.

"I don't much care where—" said Alice.

"Then it doesn't matter which way you go," said the Cat.

"—so long as I get *somewhere*," Alice added as an explanation.

"Oh, you're sure to do that," said the Cat, "if you only walk long enough."

This conversation from Lewis Carroll's 1865 classic, *Alice's Adventures in Wonderland*, illustrates the importance of knowing where you are headed. Like Alice, many organizations are uncertain where it is they want to go. As the Cheshire Cat points out, if it doesn't matter where you are going, any path will get you there.

Vision provides direction. It paints a picture of the future. It points to where the organization is going. It identifies a destination. Articulating a clear vision and gaining a sense of ownership among others is one of the most important functions of a leader.

Vision inspires confidence and courage. People can go much faster, with more confidence and courage, when they can see where they are going.

Consider the following: You are driving a car through the

mountains. Let's say you are going seventy miles per hour and it is a bright, sunny day. But suddenly, you run into a deep fog. You can barely see the road in front of you. What would be your first instinct? Most of us would hit the brakes! When you cannot see where you are going, you go slower, and with less confidence. When you can see clearly—with clear vision—you can move with speed and confidence.

VISION STATEMENTS

On May 25, 1961, President John F. Kennedy told a joint session of Congress that he envisioned "landing a man on the moon and returning him safely to the earth by the end of the decade." His vision became a reality on July 20, 1969, when Apollo 11 commander Neil Armstrong stepped onto the moon's surface. What an amazing feat!

How did this country go from lagging behind the Soviet Union in the race for space to landing a man on the moon by the end of one decade? It took great human effort and expense. Ultimately, it resulted from a vision stated in clear and certain terms that people could understand, support, and get excited about. *"Landing a man on the moon and returning him safely to the earth by the end of the decade"* meets all of the criteria for a good vision statement.

It is clear. People can understand it. No one needs to explain what it means.

It is short. A vision statement is just that—a statement. It is not a page or two of rambling paragraphs. Few will read a long vision statement. Even fewer will understand, appreciate, or remember it.

It can be accomplished. It is hard to get people behind something they know they can never achieve. A moon landing was far-reaching, but it *was* within reach.

It challenges the imagination. The vision should stretch people. It should not seem impossible to attain. Nor should it seem too easily accomplished.

It describes the future. A vision statement paints a picture of the future. It is often confused with a mission statement, which describes the present.

Vision statements often make the mistake of stating generalities like, "Be the provider of choice." Stating that your organization "will be recognized" as "a provider of choice" or "a premier organization" can make it even worse. Not only does that language suggest that recognition is more important than reality, it also takes control of your vision out of your hands and places it in the hands of those who might recognize you. Yet this is a very familiar line in vision statements.

WHY NEAR THE END OF THE PROCESS?

Though not everyone's favored approach, we prefer to discuss the organization's vision near the end of the strategic planning process.[3] Starting with a vision statement does create an end point, a destination for the process. But it is difficult for most people to articulate a vision at the beginning of the process.

The vision that is stated up front in a strategic planning process is usually the vision of one or two people, perhaps a charismatic leader. While it is important for the leaders of an organization to have a vision of the future, there is a fine line to walk here.

Strategic planning allows the opportunity for a group to create the vision together. The best leader is one who has a vision of the future, but is able to open up the conversation to the ideas and opinions of others. And in the process, what develops is a *shared vision*—not just the private vision of one or two people.

Senior authorities sometimes want to begin the strategic planning session with a description of where *they* see the organization going in the future. This is a mistake. First, it suggests that the group is dependent upon someone else, usually someone at the top of the organization, for inspiration, guidance, and direction. Second, it can stifle creative thinking about the future.

Dan was facilitating a strategic planning process for a symphony orchestra. Ten minutes before the start of the first session, the chair of the board asked Dan if they could start by asking the conductor to "share his vision of the future." Dan's response was that if the conductor spoke first, they might as well forget about the rest of the eight-hour planning process. If you start with a rousing speech about one person's vision, especially that of a charismatic figure, it will predetermine the direction for the whole strategic planning process.

Our method—which places vision toward the end of the process—is intended to *create a sense of shared vision.*[4] Once the process is complete, the vision should be clear to everyone in the room. It has been created by all of them. Now it is simply a matter of putting it into words.

We have been through strategic planning sessions where the entire first session is devoted to writing the vision statement. This can be excruciating. For all but a few people, it is like Alice in Wonderland stating her vision when she has no idea where she is going.

INTERNAL AND EXTERNAL VISION STATEMENTS

There are two types of vision statements: internal and external.[5] The internal statement describes *what the organization will look like* if the strategic plan is successfully implemented. These statements usually use words like *premier*, *best*, or *number one*. A review of vision statements shows frequent use of these words.

For example, a soft drink company might say, "Beat Pepsi." A health care system might say, "To be the premier health care system" in a region. A hotel might say, "To be the best hotel" in a given area. These internal vision statements show little imagination. They might motivate a few people inside the organization, but they do not speak to anyone else.

We prefer the *external vision statement*. It describes *how the world will be a better place because the organization succeeds* in its strategic plan. This is much more inspirational. It speaks to people inside and outside the organization.

A SIMPLE GUIDE TO WRITING THE VISION STATEMENT

We place the writing of the vision statement at the conclusion of the strategic planning process. At that point, the road map to the future has already been drawn. All that is required is for the group to put into words a description of the future success that has already been outlined in the strategic plan.

We have two ways to do the visioning process.

LONGER OPTION (ABOUT TWENTY MINUTES):

1. Ask each participant to write down a word or phrase that answers the question *"How will the world look different when your strategic plan has been fully implemented?"*
2. Ask participants for their words, and write them where they can be seen by all.
3. Ask everyone to write a sentence using these words.
4. Ask for volunteers to read their sentences aloud.
5. Ask people to comment on the sentences that appealed to them the most.

6. Test to see if there is consensus on any one of these sentences.
7. If not, test to see if a slight variation of one of them might work.
8. If necessary, designate a few people to take the results of this process and work on a draft to bring back to the group at its next meeting.

SHORTER OPTION (ABOUT TEN MINUTES):

1. Ask each participant to write down a word or phrase that answers the question "*How will the world look different when your strategic plan has been fully implemented?*"
2. Go around the room, ask the participants for their words, and write them where they can be seen by all.
3. Ask everyone to vote on which words or phrases appeal to them the most.
4. Designate a few people to take the results of this process and work on a draft to bring back to the group at its next meeting.

REALIZING THE VISION

During the first meeting of our strategic planning class, students are required to propose a destination for a class trip. They are asked to research potential destinations in advance and to come ready to convince the rest of the class their destination is the best choice.

Several interesting things typically occur. First, most students recommend going to a place they have already visited. When asked why, they say it is because they know this place, are comfortable with it, and enjoyed being there. The few students who recommend going to a place they have never been to respond to the same questions by saying things like, "Why would I want to go somewhere I've already been? I want to go to new places and learn new things."

This is very similar to the reactions of many people in organizations where the strategic plan describes a new and different vision. People often are comfortable with the status quo and do not readily embrace the notion of change. As with trying to convince students where to go for a class trip, convincing employees that a new or different direction is good for the organization can be difficult. Communication and passion are essential.

Another interesting result of the class trip exercise is that students often place unnecessary restrictions on the trip. Many recommend a destination very close to home because they fear most students would not have the time or the money for something more extravagant. Yet, we purposely do not provide any restrictions as a part of the assignment. No time frame, distance, or budget is mentioned. What if the trip took place ten years later? What if someone was willing to fund the trip?

It is human nature to place restrictions on imagination, to put up roadblocks, and to come up with reasons *not* to do something. It doesn't matter if it is a make-believe class trip exercise or real-world business.

But great organizations create a shared vision of a destination that excites people. As a result, the people involved get behind that vision. They take responsibility to help the organization get there. The key is great communication.

Fred worked for a senior authority who had just completed what he considered an exciting strategic plan. It contained some excellent recommendations and this senior authority wanted the plan to be known throughout his organization. So he told his direct reports to spread the word.

Yet, when the senior authority surveyed the workforce thirty days later, he found that only 10 percent of his workforce even knew about the strategic plan. The man was furious. He called a meeting of his direct reports and read them the riot act. How dare they not do as they were told! So he sent them on their way again, and warned them that he would survey the workforce in another thirty days.

This time, 25 percent of the organization's employees knew of the strategic plan. The senior authority was still very upset. How could this be? Were the direct reports not passing along the information? Or was the workforce just not listening?

The likely answer is a combination of each. Telling someone else to tell someone else to tell someone else is poor communication. It rarely works. Nothing is as clear and effective as personal contact.

CONCLUSION

Chad Pregracke was passionate about cleaning the Mississippi River. It was his personal vision. It spoke to him and excited him enough that he spent a full year by himself cleaning large volumes of junk out of the river. But he was also able to make the leap from one-man show to leader by sharing his vision with many others, opening himself up to the possibility that the vision might change and grow.

And grow it did. Living Lands and Waters continues to thrive because Pregracke was able to develop a team of coleaders who eventually went through our strategic planning process. Together, they created a new, shared vision and a plan to reach that vision.

A vision provides a sense of direction. It inspires courage and confidence. It can be the catalyst to get everyone moving in the same direction. It sets priorities for resource expenditures.

Visionary leaders envision the future. But they do not impose that vision upon others. They do not dictate the terms of that vision. They involve people in a participatory process, such as the one described in this book. Then they look back at the end of the process and discover what has been created. That is what we mean by cocreating the vision.

HOLD YOURSELF ACCOUNTABLE

Implement and Evaluate

"Even if you are on the right track, you will get hit by
the train if you just sit there."

—Will Rogers

We were asked by Bethany for Children and Families, a health
and human service not-for-profit, to help them to *think strategically*. We had already led them through the strategic planning
process described in this book. They were implementing the
plan and moving in a positive direction. They were tracking their
progress on action steps and were largely successful in accom-
plishing virtually everything they had set out to achieve.[1]

However, some major changes were occurring in their
environment. In response, the agency was shifting the focus of
its programs. This tested its mettle in unanticipated ways.
Program changes and adjustments raised major questions. In the
eyes of some board members, program expansion was growing
outside the agency's core mission. They were worried about *mission drift*—that is, that the agency was chasing new dollars without enough attention to whether the new programs fit its core
mission and values. As a result, the board decided to refocus
their agenda on the big picture: mission, vision, and strategy.
They needed a process to think strategically.

Like Bethany for Children and Families, many businesses are looking for ways to think strategically as an organization. It is important for leaders and managers to continuously study trends in their businesses, consider the implications of these trends, and adjust their strategies—without changing their missions, and without necessarily repeating all eight steps described in this book *every year*.

This step addresses how organizational life changes after a strategic planning process. It describes the ongoing activities that go with strategic planning: *implementation and evaluation*.

Remember: *anything worth planning is worth doing*. If you are going to spend all that time and energy doing strategic planning, it does not make sense to ignore it afterward. Yet the research shows that is exactly what most organizations do.

A SENSE OF URGENCY

Strategic planning provides an opportunity for an organization to face its current reality and to make changes to adapt to that reality.[2] Leaders must generate the interest, the energy, and the urgency for strategic planning.

The work of strategy is often seen as *important but not necessarily urgent*. Humans tend to gunnysack problems. The tendency is to drop them one by one into a sack and ignore them until, finally, a last straw explodes the whole sack. Small problems grow into major ones.

If the action steps designed in the strategic plan are indeed the most *important* work that needs to be done, does it make sense to procrastinate on working on them? The problem is that most people spend too much time on matters that are perceived as *urgent but are not necessarily important*. The key to time management is to eliminate those things in order to make more time for actions that are *important but not necessarily urgent*.

That is why leadership is so critical. Leaders change the mindset of the organization to help its members see the urgency of matters that are important. As a result, people make time for the important work that was discussed at strategic planning.

ACCOUNTABILITY SESSIONS

One way to make the action steps seem more urgent is to build accountability into the timelines set in the action steps. That is why we schedule *accountability sessions* with our clients. Usually, these are quarterly meetings of the strategic planning team. The whole team is held accountable for completing the action steps.

At the first accountability session, we look at each item that has been scheduled to be completed in three months. Most of the time, some of this work has not been done. Adrenaline was flowing at the strategic planning sessions. In the excitement of a strategic planning session, the tendency can be to shoot very high. This is not bad. In strategic planning, we step away from the urgency of the day-to-day tasks and gain more of a sense of urgency about the importance of our strategic goals. It is easy to become overly optimistic about how quickly we will take action.

We start accountability meetings by taking the blame out of the room. We set the tone for an open, honest, and candid discussion of each action item. We state upfront that by holding such an accountability session, this organization is already ahead of most.

Most organizations tend to be overly optimistic about their action steps, not realizing how difficult it will be to add this work to an already crowded list of things to do. Emergencies happen. New challenges come up every day. Even with the best intentions, we often fail to meet the planned deadlines. Tempering expectations sets the tone for a more open and honest discussion.

For each action item scheduled for completion, we ask these essential questions:

1. Was this action item completed?
   a. *If the answer is yes*: What is the next step in moving toward the strategy for this action item? What is the timeline for that step and who will be held accountable for it?
   b. *If the answer is no*: Does this action step still need to be completed?
      i. If yes, when will it be completed? Does it need to be changed?
      ii. If no, what alternative action will move us toward the strategy listed above this action step?
2. Does the completion or deletion of this action step alter anything else on this strategic plan? Does it require any change in the strategies?

Work item by item through the whole plan to evaluate, discuss, reconsider, change, and update the strategic plan based on this process.

Schedule another accountability session for the six-month review. At six, nine, and twelve months, go through the same set of questions.

In order for this evaluative process to work, the action plan needs to be specific, realistic, and timely—with a timeline and contact person assigned to each action step. When we get to the accountability session, there can be no doubt as to who is going to report on each action step, when the step was supposed to be completed, and whether the expected action was taken or not.

When organizations assign actions that are hard to measure, it decreases the likelihood of implementation because it gets too complicated to figure out whether the plan is being implemented or not.

Specificity leads to measurability, which leads to accountability.

STRATEGIC THINKING

Strategic planning should be seen as more than a one-time event. Once the strategic planning process is finished, the plan needs to be implemented, evaluated, and adjusted. The people involved in planning need to continue to think strategically.

Strategic planning is necessary but not sufficient. Planning is rational, intentional, and formal.[3] It is limited to a specific time and place. It needs to be complemented by strategic thinking. The strategic plan needs to become a living document that is updated as changes occur.

Strategic planning assumes that environmental changes— those happening beyond your control—are continuous. The pace, direction, and intensity of those changes will continue to shift after the strategic planning process has been completed. Even the most forward-looking of leaders can miss some of the environmental changes that may occur *after* the strategic planning sessions.

Consider a football team. Strategic planning is how the coaches prepare before the game. But once the game begins, the team needs to make adjustments. When the wind shifts direction, a key player gets hurt, or the competition tries an unanticipated attack, the team needs to adjust the game plan. This is what we mean by *strategic thinking*.

Strategic thinking requires continuous thinking, reflecting, learning, and asking the right questions about the ongoing changes in your external environment. It requires hindsight, insight, and foresight. You need hindsight into the significant events of the past, insight into the present, and foresight to anticipate the significant future events.

Strategic thinking among leaders and managers is just as important as selecting the right strategy during the strategic planning process. The strategy will need to be adjusted regularly. Flexibility becomes important so the organization does not bog down in bureaucratic processes and fail to change direction when it becomes critically important.

Too often, the separation of strategic planning from strategic thinking begins with the separation of those who plan from those who implement. If we expect leaders and followers, managers and workers to be involved in implementation, we need to involve them in the planning and the thinking process. We believe it is important to involve doers and visionaries—those who implement and those who dream—in strategic planning and its implementation.

You need the *idealism* of leaders and the *realism* of managers. Leaders can dream idealistically about ways to adjust, adapt, and grow into the future. Managers can help make those dreams a reality.

THINKING STRATEGICALLY AS AN ORGANIZATION

Changes that occur in organizational life can be harder to see and adjust to than those on a football field. Few are trained to think strategically, to see the big picture, and to anticipate the next set of big changes in their external environments—those outside their control.

With any group, a core leadership principle is *start where people are at that moment*. Working with the board and staff at Bethany for Children and Families, we developed the following five-step process, which begins with figuring out how much people already know.

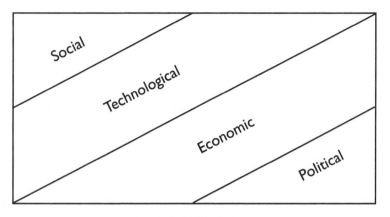

Figure 7: STEP Analysis

A FIVE-STEP STRATEGIC THINKING PROCESS

First, interview your people to find out how much they already know about the changes and trends in your business. You can frame your interview questions around a STEP (*Social, Technological, Economic*, and *Political*) Analysis:

- *Social changes*: What social changes are occurring locally, regionally, and globally that affect you, your business, and your market? Think about family and community patterns, cultural shifts, and demographic changes.
- *Technological changes*: What technological changes are occurring locally, regionally, and globally that affect you, your business, and your market? Include social media, information technology, and other communication trends and changes.
- *Economic changes*: What economic changes are occurring locally, regionally, and globally that affect you, your business, and your market? Consider family income,

unemployment trends, insurance rates, or health care costs.

- *Political changes*: What political changes are occurring locally, regionally, and globally that affect you, your business, and your market? Review public opinion polls, partisan changes, policy changes, or attitudes toward government.

Second, find out what you are missing. When looking at these trends, what questions emerge? What trends seem exciting...or troubling? Which trends are most relevant to your future? This is a time to go back to the research methods described in Step Two and do another round of study. This might include interviews, surveys, focus groups, strategic assessments, and literature searches.

Third, narrow the scope of your analysis: What are the emerging needs, issues, and concerns in your business—and your market—that are not being addressed? What are the unsponsored needs, those not being met by others? And what are the primary sponsored needs? Which of these is a priority? Which of these makes the most sense for you to address?

The core of this step is discovering your *strategic competitive advantage* (SCA).[4] Your SCA is what gives you an advantage over similar organizations or competitors. Look at how your internal strengths and weaknesses match up with the external opportunities and threats in your environment.

The *hedgehog concept* is a similar concept (see Figure 8).[5] This tool suggests that organizations prioritize activities that fit the intersection between three criteria:

- Mission—what are you passionate about?
- Competencies—what do you excel at?
- Money—what can be profitable?

If you can find projects, programs, products, or services that fit these three criteria, you can narrow the scope of your search for priorities.

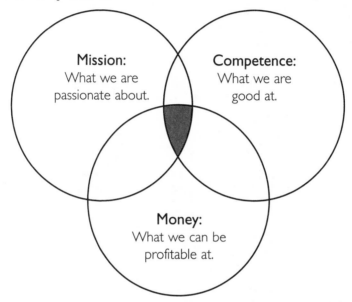

Figure 8: Hedgehog Concept

Fourth, develop a course of action for your priority issues: What can you do in the strategic sense? How can you capitalize on your SCA? How can you position yourself to meet the needs identified above? Make sure any action steps you decide upon are measurable, with a timeline and key contact persons assigned to each step.

Fifth, look at making updates to your strategic plan. Consider whether you need to change any strategic goals or strategies in your strategic plan. If you add a strategic goal, consider the possibility of archiving another one. Add specific action steps with timelines, contact persons, and accountability built into them.

ONGOING AND CONTINUOUS

Our five-step strategic thinking process can complement the process described in this book. In the years that you decide not to go through the full process of strategic planning—the eight steps described in this book—you might be interested in using the five-step strategic thinking process instead.

We have found that implementation and evaluation, when done well, will lead to strategic thinking. Strategic thinking, when done well, will lead to the update of your strategic plan. The organization that implements, evaluates, and revises their strategic plan will be forced to *think* strategically.

The Five-Step Strategic Thinking Process
Find out what your people know.
Conduct research to further that understanding.
Narrow the scope of your analysis to priority issues.
Take action steps that move your business in the right direction.
Adjust your strategic plan accordingly.

This process can be used as an ongoing process of strategic thinking or an alternative way to update your strategic plan.

Generally speaking, we recommend a full strategic planning process about every two to three years. In the alternate years—when you decide not to complete the full process—you need to continue to think strategically and update your strategic plan accordingly. Whatever form strategic leadership takes, it needs to be ongoing and continuous because external change is ongoing and continuous.

AN ANNUAL RETREAT: THE PLANNING CENTER

One organization that has learned to do this well is The Planning Center. Dan has facilitated their strategic planning process on several occasions. They hold accountability sessions regularly to evaluate and update their plan.[6]

About three years into their process, the leaders at The Planning Center asked Dan to facilitate their annual retreat. At this retreat, they would

1. Identify and celebrate milestones for each member of the staff;
2. Review the major news events at the local, national, and international levels;
3. Tell stories that capture the core values they espouse;
4. Imagine what they would look like if they grew ten times (10X) over ten years;
5. Identify opportunities and roadblocks to growing ten times (10X);
6. Conduct a STEP Analysis and a new SWOT; and
7. Review and revise the strategic plan accordingly.

As with most retreats of this type, The Planning Center also spends considerable time building relationships among the staff, particularly new employees. As they are growing, it is critically important that new members of the team are committed to the core values, understand the strategic direction, and are involved in imagining the future of The Planning Center.

ADAPTIVE CHANGE

Another aspect of strategic leadership that involves responding to strategic challenges is what Ronald Heifetz has called *adaptive change*.[7] Heifetz suggests that we need to distinguish between technical change and adaptive change. Technical issues have technical solutions. They can be frustrating. But compared to adaptive issues, they are easy to fix.

Adaptive issues require adaptive solutions: Customers no longer buy our product. Banks no longer loan us money. Suppliers no longer provide a resource we need. Employees are leaving in large numbers. Policies followed for decades no longer work.

Adaptive issues are the ones that need attitudinal or behavioral change. Heifetz describes this as *leadership without easy answers*.

Adaptive change demands hard work. It requires changes in personal attitudes and organizational behaviors. It requires that the people in the organization *adapt* to external changes going on in the world by making internal changes in attitudes and behaviors.

For example, the profitability of an engineering company was jeopardized by a new process of bidding for contracts. This change required engineers to learn to collaborate with contractors of many different types in order to submit joint proposals under a general contractor. If the engineers could not develop these skills, the company could go out of business.

This is a life-threatening adaptive challenge. Bidding on contracts is the company's lifeblood. The complex people skills involved in negotiation, communication, and collaboration—not previously a part of the skill set required of engineers—will become a necessary addition to their skill set for the company to stay in business. When you convince others to face the reality of adaptive challenges like this, you are practicing adaptive leadership.

Most issues require a combination of technical and adaptive solutions. Technical issues can have adaptive components or develop into adaptive issues if they become repeated problems. The problem is that we often look only for a technical solution to something that requires both an adaptive and technical solution.

If we only solve the technical side of our adaptive issues, then problems will compound. They will not go away. Adaptive issues create a need for internal change to adjust to the external change occurring in your environment. Adaptive issues present a call for leadership. Adaptive leaders change attitudes, thinking, and behaviors. They change strategy, structure, and culture.[8]

CONCLUSION

The leaders and managers of Bethany for Children and Families were looking for something to go beyond the eight steps described in this book. They realized that strategic planning was just a starting point for strategic leadership.

Their call led us to creating the five-step strategic thinking process described in this chapter. It offers structure to the ongoing need for strategic thinking.

Strategic planning identifies our priority needs, issues, and actions. When the process is completed, the action steps identified should become the first priorities on your to-do list. The leaders in the organization must insist on it. They *create a sense of urgency about what is important.*

Strategic leaders hold the organization accountable for continuously implementing and evaluating the strategic plan. Without constant internal changes, your organization will not survive the entropic forces that threaten your livelihood and demand continuous growth, development, and change.

CONCLUSION

A Call for Strategic Leadership

"The future ain't what it used to be."

—Yogi Berra

There is no substitute for leadership. We have made many suggestions about how to increase the likelihood of implementation, but without a leader who can inspire, motivate, and encourage people to stay focused, your strategic plan may be lost on a hard drive.

We believe that it is necessary for most organizations to go through a formal process of strategic planning every two or three years, depending on the amount of volatility in their environment. The more change is occurring, the more you need to plan strategically.

Strategic planning is necessary, but planning alone is not sufficient. Organizations need both strategic planning *and* strategic thinking. Remember the following:

> *Strategic planning* is the formal process of focusing energy toward strategy.
> *Strategic thinking* is the ongoing work of strategy.
> *Strategic leadership* is the combination of strategic planning *and* strategic thinking.

WHITE WATER RAFTING

The old metaphor for strategic work was a mountaintop retreat, where the organization's top leaders and managers would get away for a few days of strategic planning. They would set goals for the next three to five years and then come down from the mountain to tell the people where the organization would be heading for that period. Sounds simple.

The new metaphor for strategic work is *white water rafting.* Everyone is in the same boat together, each with a separate role, moving swiftly through dangerous waters, twisting and turning to stay on course, shifting their attention from one new challenge to another, trusting each other to make quick decisions, and sometimes placing their lives in the hands of others. In this fast-moving raft, levels of trust, commitment, and cohesion are critical. Decisions are made quickly based on simple rules, core values, and advance planning. This is the new reality in a world of constant change.

This new reality requires *strategic leadership*. Organizational leaders must think constantly about strategy and be proactive as they adapt to changes in their external environment.

BENEFITS OF STRATEGIC PLANNING

Each step in our process provides benefits to your organization:

1. The *environmental assessment* provides feedback and input from many stakeholders, data about your strengths and weaknesses, and identifiable trends in your business.
2. The *strategic goals* identified through our process provide a framework for thinking strategically about your future. They become the agenda for meetings of your leadership team.
3. The strategic planning *process* brings your whole team together and builds social capital. Building consensus around strategy can be a team-building exercise.
4. The strategic planning *product* is a guide for measuring how your organization is doing. It is a roadmap with specific steps, targets, and benchmarks.
5. The *action plan* gives you something specific to begin working on right away. It becomes the framework for holding people accountable for the plan.
6. The *whole experience* of strategic planning enables you to be more prepared to take advantage of new opportunities that appear in the future or new threats that need to be confronted.
7. In short, strategic planning develops your capacity to do the ongoing and continuous work of *strategic thinking*.

PITFALLS OF STRATEGIC PLANNING

Each step in our process has inherent obstacles and challenges:

1. Political agendas can get in the way of honest debate and healthy dialogue about the strategic goals facing your organization.
2. Those in positions of authority can undermine the process if they are not highly involved, committed, and supportive about allocating the resources needed for implementation.
3. It is important to involve a good mix of managers and leaders on your strategic planning team. Managers can provide a reality check about what can and cannot be done.
4. Without the specificity of an action plan, the strategic plan lacks accountability. As a result, the strategic plan often goes without implementation.
5. Communication and involvement needs to be both bottom-up and top-down.

REPERCUSSIONS OF NOT PLANNING

Some organizations are suffering from a lack of strategic leadership. They neither plan nor think strategically. Signs of this type of organization include the following:

1. The leaders and managers are not on the same page about what is important.
2. The organization seems to move from one initiative to another without making progress.
3. Team members are frustrated as they seem to be going through the motions.

4. The organization is losing ground to its competition.

5. Team members are not adapting to the changes in their external environment.

6. Unless the organization changes course, it will go out of business.

LIMITATIONS OF STRATEGIC PLANNING

Strategic *planning* is only a starting point. It emphasizes the formal, rational, and intentional process of planning for strategic direction. In times of volatile change, the strategic *thinking* demands of leadership can become even more critical. You need to adjust to external changes on the fly and develop emergent strategies—ones that become apparent after the strategic planning process.

Strategic planning is limited by the amount of time, attention, resources, communication, and participation of the organization. To minimize the impact of these limitations, you need to

- Recruit an effective strategic planning team to guide the process;
- Get the right players to the table;
- Designate key roles and responsibilities;
- Identify someone to facilitate the process;
- Involve people to get buy-in;
- Do enough homework to conduct the environmental assessment;
- Have the discipline to keep the plan doable;
- Line up the resources needed for implementation; and
- Keep strategy front and center for the organizational leaders and managers.

Strategic plans are only as good as the time, energy, and resources that people put into them. They rise or fall based on the strength of the hindsight, insight, and foresight of the leaders, managers, and participants on the strategic planning team.

While leadership may come from a person in a position of authority, the leadership activities described in this book do not require positional authority. In short, leadership is not a position. It is not a rank. Leadership does take an incredible amount of humility, courage, and openness to new ideas.[1]

Viewed this way, strategic leadership can emerge from anyone involved in the strategic planning process—not only from those in positions of authority. Anyone with the hindsight, insight, and foresight to affect the strategic planning team can engage in leadership. Therefore, those in authority need to be willing to invite people throughout the organization to participate in some way, and be willing to listen to their input.

WHAT MAKES AN EFFECTIVE STRATEGIC PLAN?

The first measure of a good strategic plan is that the change is significant and moves the organization in the direction of a *shared* vision. Vision is about direction. The strategic plan is the most comprehensive statement about the future direction of the organization. It addresses the most critical strategic areas with strategies that will work.

The second measure of an effective strategic plan is that it gets *implemented*. It is shocking to see how many organizations develop a strategic plan but fail to implement it. Each step in our interactive process helps to enhance the likelihood of implementation.

The third measure of a good strategic plan is *consensus*. Engaging as many stakeholders as possible in the strategic planning process is essential to creating ownership of the eventual plan. People will feel a sense of shared vision when they are cocreators of the plan. We have many ways to involve large numbers of people in various steps of the strategic planning process. Involving others helps them to buy into—and gain ownership of—the plan.

The benefits of formal strategic planning far outweigh the limitations. Change is perpetual. The pace of change is rapidly increasing. Therefore, strategic thinking is becoming ever more critical. We believe that strategic planning, when coupled with the ongoing work of strategic thinking, implementation, and evaluation, provides a framework for *strategic leadership*.

**Visit our website at
www.strategicplanningforleaders.com.**

NOTES

INTRODUCTION

1. Robert R. Blake and Jane S. Mouton, *The Managerial Grid: Key Orientations for Achieving Production through People* (Houston: Gulf Publishing, 1964).

2. John P. Kotter, *Leading Change* (Boston: Harvard Business School Press, 1996).

3. Joseph C. Rost, *Leadership for the Twenty-First Century* (New York: Praeger, 1991).

STEP ONE

1. For the full story on The Crawford Company, as well as their core values statement, visit their website at www.crawford-company.com.

2. Dan R. Ebener, *Servant Leadership Models for Your Parish* (Mahwah, NJ: Paulist Press, 2010).

3. Sample copies of mission, vision, and values statements, as well as a template for contracting with a strategic planning facilitator, are included on our website at www.strategicplanningforleaders.com.

4. For more information about the Davenport Fire Department, go to www.cityofdavenportiowa.com.

STEP TWO

1. Ronald A. Heifetz and Martin Linsky, *Leadership on the Line: Staying Alive Through the Dangers of Leading* (Boston: Harvard Business School Press, 2002).

2. J. Edward Russo and Paul J. H. Schoemaker, *Winning Decisions: Getting It Right the First Time* (New York: Doubleday, 2002).

3. Donald T. Campbell and Julian C. Stanley, *Experimental and Quasi-Experimental Designs for Research* (Boston: Houghton Mifflin, 1963); and Thomas W. Mangione, *Mail Surveys: Improving the Quality* (Thousand Oaks, CA: Sage Publications, 1995).

4. David W. Stewart and Prem N. Shamdasani, *Focus Groups: Theory and Practice* (Newbury Park, CA: Sage Publications, 1990).

5. View our full guide to facilitation on our website at www.strategicplanningforleaders.com.

STEP THREE

1. For more information about Medic EMS, go to www.medi cems.com.

2. Edgar H. Schein, *Organizational Culture and Leadership*, 3rd ed. (San Francisco: Jossey-Bass, 2002).

3. Michael Allison and Jude Kaye, *Strategic Planning for Nonprofit Organizations: A Practical Guide and Workbook* (Hoboken, NJ: John Wiley & Sons, 2005).

4. Peter C. Brinckerhoff, *Mission-Based Management: Leading Your Not-for-Profit into the 21st Century* (Dillon, CO: Alpine Guild, 1994).

5. Bernard M. Bass, "From Transactional to Transformational Leadership: Sharing the Vision," *Organizational Dynamics* 18, no. 3 (1990): 19–31.

6. Dennis W. Organ, *Organizational Citizenship Behavior: The Good Soldier Syndrome* (Lexington, MA: Lexington Books, 1988).

7. For more information on the Girl Scouts of Western Illinois and Eastern Iowa, including their mission, vision, and values statements, go to www.girlscoutstoday.org.

8. To get a copy of our full list of possible core values for this process, visit our website at www.strategicplanningforleaders.com.

9. For more information on the Nominal Group Technique, visit our website at www.strategicplanningforleaders.com.

10. For more information on Family Resources Inc., including their mission, vision, and values statements, go to www.famres.org.

STEP FOUR

1. Russo and Schoemaker, *Winning Decisions*.

2. Henry Mintzberg, Bruce W. Ahlstrand, and Joseph Lampel, *Strategy Safari: A Guided Tour through the Wilds of Strategic Management* (New York: Free Press, 1998).

3. For more information on the MacMillan Matrix, visit our website at www.strategicplanningforleaders.com.

4. John M. Bryson, *Strategic Planning for Public and Nonprofit Organizations: A Guide to Strengthening and Sustaining Organizational Achievement*, 3rd ed. (San Francisco: Jossey-Bass, 2004).

5. Ibid.

STEP FIVE

1. John P. Kotter, *A Sense of Urgency* (Boston: Harvard Business School Press, 2008).

2. President Dwight Eisenhower is credited with popularizing this notion of focusing on things that are "*important but not urgent.*" He suggested that people need to minimize the amount of time spent on matters that are "*urgent but not important.*" Many other authors have used a similar model.

3. We have some materials about consensus, including what it is and how it is reached, on our website at www.strategicplanningfor leaders.com.

STEP SIX

1. We have seen dozens of sources that suggest that somewhere between 70 and 90 percent of strategic plans are not implemented. For example, Bridges Better Consultancy International Research states that 90 percent of strategic plans are not implemented successfully. Mintzberg, Ahlstrand, and Lampel (1998) cite similar statistics.

2. To view some sample dashboards, visit our website at www.strategicplanningforleaders.com.

3. K. A. Jehn and E. A. Mannix, "The Dynamic Nature of Conflict: A Longitudinal Study of Intragroup Conflict and Group Performance," *Academy of Management Journal* 44, no. 2 (2001): 238–51.

4. Ibid.

5. Ibid.

6. K. W. Thomas, "Conflict and Negotiation Processes in Organizations," in *Handbook of Industrial and Organizational Psychology*, 2nd ed., ed. M. D. Dunnette and L. M. Hough (Palo Alto, CA: Consulting Psychologists Press, 1992), 3:651–717.

7. There are many sources that deal with this subject but the classic is Roger Fisher, William Ury, and Bruce Patton, *Getting to YES: Negotiating Agreement without Giving In* (New York: Penguin Books, 1991).

STEP SEVEN

1. For more information on the work of Chad Pregracke and Living Lands and Waters, visit their website at www.livinglandsandwaters.org.

2. James M. Kouzes and Barry Z. Posner, *The Leadership Challenge: How to Keep Getting Extraordinary Things Done in Organizations* (San Francisco: Jossey-Bass, 2003).

3. Bryson, *Strategic Planning*.

4. Kouzes and Posner, *The Leadership Challenge*.

5. Bryson, *Strategic Planning*.

STEP EIGHT

1. For more information on Bethany for Children and Families, go to www.bethany-qc.org.

2. Dean Williams, *Real Leadership: Helping People and Organizations Face Their Toughest Challenges* (San Francisco: Berrett-Koehler, 2005).

3. Mintzberg, Ahlstrand, and Lampel, *Strategy Safari*.

4. Michael E. Porter, *Competitive Strategy: Techniques for Analyzing Industry and Competitors* (New York: Free Press, 1980).

5. James C. Collins, *Good to Great: Why Some Companies Make the Leap and Others Don't* (New York: HarperCollins, 2001).

6. For more information on The Planning Center, go to www.theplanningcenter.com.

7. Ronald A. Heifetz, *Leadership without Easy Answers* (Cambridge, MA: Belknap Press of Harvard University Press, 1995).

8. Ronald A. Heifetz and Martin Linsky, *Leadership on the Line: Staying Alive through the Dangers of Leading* (Boston: Harvard Business School Press, 2002).

CONCLUSION

1. Dan R. Ebener, *Blessings for Leaders: Leadership Wisdom from the Beatitudes* (Collegeville, MN: Liturgical Press, 2012).

ACKNOWLEDGMENTS

To the hundreds of MOL students in our strategic planning classes who provided feedback on early versions of this book and have taught us as much as we have taught them;

To the thousands of participants in our strategic planning sessions who allowed us to experience, test, and improve the process described in this book;

To Craig DeVrieze of St. Ambrose University and Mark Ridolfi of the *Quad City Times*, for editing early versions of this book;

To Randy Richards, Ron Wastyn, Rick Dienesch, Megan Gisi, George Hollins, and all our colleagues at St. Ambrose University, for the ongoing dialogue about leadership;

To our colleagues in strategic planning, especially Linda Wastyn, Kevin James, Steve Ambrozi, Laura Beason, Diane Fall, Luke Ebener, Kelly Dybvig, and Danielle Ebaugh;

To Laurie Hoefling of the Diocese of Davenport for her technical support;

To Jordan Kremer for youthful enthusiasm about the website;

To Paulist Press for their collegiality in publishing this book;

And Most of All: To our wives, DeAnn Stone Ebener and Kerry Lynn Smith, for their enduring love and support, and to whom this book is dedicated.